Passports to Literacy
Words 2

Gillian Brown and Kate Ruttle

General Editors

Richard Brown
and Kate Ruttle

Consultant Editor

Jean Glasberg

CAMBRIDGE
UNIVERSITY PRESS

PUBLISHED BY THE PRESS SYNDICATE OF THE UNIVERSITY OF CAMBRIDGE
The Pitt Building, Trumpington Street, Cambridge CB2 1RP, United Kingdom

CAMBRIDGE UNIVERSITY PRESS
The Edinburgh Building, Cambridge CB2 2RU, United Kingdom
40 West 20th Street, New York, NY 10011-4211, USA
10 Stamford Road, Oakleigh, Melbourne 3166, Australia

Passports to Literacy
Words 2
Text © Gillian Brown and Kate Ruttle 1998

First published 1998

Printed in the United Kingdom at the University Press, Cambridge

A catalogue record for this book is available from the British Library

ISBN 0 521 64808 4

Prepared for publication by Paren & Stacey Editorial Consultants

Design by Design/Section, Frome

Phonics for Reading by Gillian Brown and Kate Ruttle, referred to in the Introduction
for teachers, gives further practice in recognition of spelling patterns at the Towards
Independence phase of **Cambridge Reading** (ISBN 0 521 55966 9)

Contents

PART ONE: Introduction to teachers

Introduction

How to use this book

General games

PART TWO: Word games and instructions

The relationship of each unit to the National Literary Strategy guidelines is indicated by the numbers following the title (e.g.in NLS 4.3.1, 4 indicates the year, 3 the term, and 1 the NLS guidance point). Most numbers refer to the Word level work guidance, but occasional cross-reference is also made to the guidance on Sentence level work.

PART ONE:
Introduction to teachers

Introduction

The aims of the book

This book has four main aims:

◆ to develop children's ability to cope with common spelling patterns, including exceptions to normal sound–spelling regularities

◆ to develop children's ability to write plurals, past tenses, etc. correctly, and to recognise regular relationships between word classes (nouns, verbs and adjectives)

◆ to develop children's ability to recognise patterns of word meaning and to extend their vocabulary

◆ to do all this in the context of structured, motivating and enjoyable games.

A good deal of the work of the National Literacy Framework can only be done in the context of the children's ongoing writing activities. What this book offers is an opportunity for the children to reinforce many of the skills needed in developing literacy, for instance developing the ability to spell by analogy with other known words.

The organisation of this book

Introductory sections

A general outline of this book is followed by a brief discussion of non-standard accents. Then comes a section called 'Spelling rules for adding suffixes' (page 10), which covers most of the spelling rules needed for this book.

Some aspects of spelling and word-making suggested by the National Literacy Framework for Year 4 do not fit comfortably into the game format. We discuss these in 'Covering word level work' (page 11).

This is followed by 'How to use this book', which outlines in detail how a learning session might be organised.

The final part of these introductory sections, 'General games', provides brief descriptions of further word-games which can be used to familiarise children with spelling rules and conventions and to enlarge their vocabularies.

Activities

The activities are organised into three main sections:
Section 1: Spelling conventions and rules
Section 2: Spelling conventions and rules: word making
Section 3: Vocabulary extension: word meaning

Within each of the three main sections, the activities are organised so that they begin with word patterns which the children are likely to be most familiar with (particularly if they have already completed the activities in *Words 1*). Later activities in each section build on the earlier work. There is no progression between Sections 1, 2 and 3 so children could, for instance, work on the first two activities in Section 1 and then move on to the first activities in Sections 2 and 3, before returning to Section 1.

Section 1: Spelling conventions and rules

The first section begins by revising alphabetical order, since children need to be competent in looking up words in the dictionary if they are to check their spellings in the activities which follow.

Game 3 revises and develops work on the essential differences between short and long vowels. Short vowels are the ones in words like *pit, pet, pat, pot, putt* and *put*, whose spelling is mostly straightforward. The other vowels are an assorted bunch all called 'long vowels'. They occur (for most accents) in words like *bee, bay, buy, boy, bough, tow, two, beer, bare, bar, bore, boor, burr*. The spelling patterns associated with long vowels are quite varied. Different ways of spelling long vowels are explored here in Games 4 and 9 and throughout the *Words* series (see also *Phonics for Reading*).

Section 2: Spelling conventions and rules: word making

Section 2 looks at various rules and conventions governing the ways in which bits of words can be put together to create different word forms. We begin with the notion of the base form of the word. The base form of the word is the simplest form of the word, the form that you would find as the main entry in a dictionary. The base form of nouns (for example, *egg, baby, car*) can have endings added to give plural forms or possessive forms.

Similarly the base form of a verb (the so-called 'infinitive' form, for example *know, hit, have, be*) can have various endings added to give the past tense form, the *-ing* form, and so on. The base form of adjectives, with comparative and superlative endings, is dealt with in Game 19. (The relationships between nouns, verbs and adjectives and their various endings are explored in detail in *Sentences 2*.)

Throughout this book there are likely to be new words appearing in some games which are not familiar to all the children. One of the aims of the book is to help to extend the children's vocabulary. When a new word is encountered, the children should see if anyone else knows what it means, and then check in the dictionary. They should immediately use the word in a sentence, making sure the sentence makes sense, writing down the word in their vocabulary books so that they remember the spelling. Ideally you would recycle each week's crop of new words a week or so later, to help the children remember them.

This section explores the relationships between word meanings in particular areas of vocabulary. Game 28 is intended to develop the children's ability to use definitions to help them identify a word – this is simply one instance of what needs to be part of the ongoing activity of the literacy hour. The section is also concerned to identify the different spellings of words which sound the same but have very different meanings (for example, *two, too, to*).

Accents

In all work on sound–spelling relationships it is important to be sensitive to the possibility of children's accents differing from those of other children in the class, or from your own. The most striking differences between English accents are found between those who do and those who do not pronounce the 'r' anywhere where you have a spelling sequence vowel + *r* (for example, words like *door, fear, car, tyre*). R-pronouncing speakers may come from Scotland, Ireland, the southwest of England, and from North America. But in addition to the *r*-pronouncing versus non-*r*-pronouncing accents, there are many other regional variations, for example whether or not you pronounce *class* with the same vowel that you use in *pat*, and whether or not you have different vowels in *put* and *putt* (many speakers in the Midlands and Yorkshire, for instance, pronounce those words identically). If you find that a child's accent doesn't fit into the pattern which a particular activity expects, don't hesitate to adjust the materials to fit the child.

Spelling rules for adding suffixes

The rules suggested below are not adequate for the whole of the English language! They relate to the spelling patterns in the activities in this book, and they are arranged so that they relate to particular games. This means there is some repetition of details.

Adding suffixes to words ending in -y

(i) If the word is spelt with a vowel before *-y* as in *stay, play, toy*, simply add the suffixes *-s*, *-ed*, *-ing*, etc.:
stay+s stay+ed stay+ing play+ed play+ing toy+s

(ii) If the word is spelt with a consonant before *-y* as in *cry, marry*, simply leave the *-y* before *-ing* (otherwise you'd have two *i*'s together which English spelling never has):
cry+ing   marry+ing   supply+ing

(iii) But, <u>in general</u>, if the word is spelt with a consonant before *-y*, change the *-y* to *-i* before you add plural, past tense and other suffixes (see the table below).

<u>Note</u> that the plural and the third person singular suffixes after *-i-* are spelt *-es* (past tense is still *-ed*).

Base form	Plural	She/he/it	Past tense	Adjective
cry		*cri+es*	*cri+ed*	
hurry		*hurri+es*	*hurri+ed*	
supply		*suppli+es*	*suppli+ed*	
city	*citi+es*			
baby	*babi+es*			
story	*stori+es*			
beauty				*beauti+ful*
pity		*piti+es*	*piti+ed*	*piti+ful*

<u>Note</u> that the comparative and superlative forms of adjectives also change *-y* to *-i-*:

funny   funni+er   funni+est
happy   happi+er   happi+est

General rules for adding suffixes -ed and -ing to verbs

(i) If the verb ends with more than one consonant, simply add the suffix:
sniff+ing   climb+ing   wish+ing   pull+ing watch+ing
sniff+ed   climb+ed   wish+ed   pull+ed watch+ed

(ii) If the verb has a short vowel and ends with a single consonant, double the consonant and add the suffix:

knit+t+ing   wrap+p+ing   scrub+b+ing
hum+m+ing
knit+t+ed   wrap+p+ed   scrub+b+ed
hum+m+ed

(iii) If the verb ends with an *-e*, take off the *-e* and add *-ing*. For the past tense suffix, just add *-d*:

scar+ing   hop+ing   clos+ing   smil+ing
scare+d   hope+d   close+d   smile+d

(iv) If the verb ends in consonant + *-y*, leave the *-y* and just add *-ing*. Change *-y* to *-i-* before adding the past tense suffix *-d*:

reply+ing   cry+ing   marry+ing
repli+ed   cri+ed   marri+ed

(v) If the verb ends in a vowel + *-y*, simply add the suffix:

stay+ing   play+ing
stay+ed   play+ed

Note that *pay* and *say* are exceptions to this rule, and turn *-y* to *-i-* before the suffix *-d*:

pay+ing   say+ing
pai+d   sai+d

Verb forms in third person singular and noun plurals

(i) If the word ends with a 'hissing' consonant, add the suffix *-es*:

bus+es   kiss+es   box+es   match+es
buzz+es   bush+es   lunch+es   atlas+es
crush+es

(ii) If the word ends with consonant + *-y*, change *-y* to *-i-* and add the suffix *-es*.

cri+es   tri+es   stori+es   citi+es

(iii) Otherwise just add the suffix *-s*:

book+s   letter+s   sausage+s   hand+s
toe+s   piano+s   play+s   run+s

<u>*Do not use an apostrophe for any plural*</u> unless the plural is indicating possession as in *the doctors' patients*. (See rules for using apostrophes in the Introduction to *Words 1* and Units 16 and 24 in *Sentences 2*.)

Words with suffixes -able, -ation, -ion, -al

(i) If the word ends in consonant + *-y*, change *-y* to *-i-*:

reli-able   deni-al   deni-able   tri-al

(ii) If the word ends in *-e*, take off the *-e* before adding the suffix:

us+able   desir+able   believ+able   ador+able
(Exceptions: *agree+able, notice+able, like+able*)

calculat+ion   observ+ation   invit+ation
examin+ation   separat+ion   relat+ion
remov+al   arriv+al   surviv+al

(iii) Otherwise just add the suffix to the base form:

break+able   fashion+able   drink+able
enjoy+able   alter+ation   instruct+ion
except+ion+al   connect+ion   convict+ion

Covering word level work: spelling, etc.

Some aspects of the National Literacy Framework do not lend themselves to presentation within a games format but need to be incorporated either within ongoing work patterns, or dealt with in short 5–10-minute slots as an issue arises in the course of reading.

Dictionaries and thesauruses are valuable tools in the classroom and children need to get used to handling them confidently and quickly. We do offer one exercise specifically on alphabetisation (Game 1) and one on definitions (Game 28), but children need constant practice with these. They may also need to be reminded several times just how to use the particular thesaurus which you have.

Rhyming dictionaries are not only useful for making rhymes, jingles, etc. but also to look up different types of word endings (suffixes) to see how many words with a particular ending the children know. If, for instance, you look at suffixes like *-ate, -ify, -en, -ise* you will find rather advanced words like *fixate, simplify, solidify, deaden* and *dramatise*. Only a few of these seem appropriate for use with 8–9-year-olds (see NLS Framework page 39, Words point 14).

The games in this book include many, but not all, of the words which the National Literacy Framework proposes that Year 4 children should be able to read and spell correctly. It is likely that most of the remaining words will be encountered during the course of the year's reading, which is the most natural environment to meet new words. You would need to check towards the end of the year to see if any words on this list are still unfamiliar.

It is also in the course of reading that children are most likely to encounter old-fashioned words which are no longer commonly used: *frock, bathing costume, wireless, gramophone, telegram, half-a-crown, gosh, liberty bodice, compartment* (in a train), *station master*, etc.

As they arise, discuss with the children why the term has changed. Is it because some feature of life has disappeared (*telegram, half-a-crown, liberty bodice*)? Or because something has been modernised and changed (*wireless, gramophone*)? Or simply because the fashionable name has changed (*frock, bathing costume, station master*)?

Can the children think of items they may have known or still know whose names may disappear from common use (*milk bottle, post mistress, typewriter, half p, yards, feet and inches*)? Can they think of very recent words which have come into the language (computer terms, slang, exclamations of pleasure, disgust or surprise: *hypertext, cyberspace*, etc.)? Do they also know some grammatical words (like *thee, thou*) which may still be found in some dialects but have restricted use (mostly in old-fashioned church services) in modern English?

A number of issues introduced in the guidance for Word level work in the National Literacy Framework, for instance the spelling of possessive pronouns like *ours, yours* and *its*, and the use of apostrophes, is discussed in detail in several units in *Sentences 2*, where the issues arise in looking at particular texts. Seeing these forms being used meaningfully in a context should help the children to fix in memory the different meanings and usages.

How to use this book

The games in this book are intended to reinforce, and give opportunities to practise, skills and knowledge which have already been taught. Whether children have been introduced to letter patterns and word-making strategies through activities such as those described in this book, or the letter patterns and word meanings have been introduced in a short session just before the children play the games, the games should not be regarded as the principal teaching resource. There are many links with activities in *Sentences 2*, where a structured teaching sequence is suggested.

Once the children understand the spelling, word-making or word-meaning principle involved in the game, they should be able to play it independently. On each double-page spread, most of the left-hand page is written for the children to read and gives:

◆ details of what is needed to prepare and play the game

◆ detailed instructions on how to play the game

◆ guidance on how to decide who has won

◆ relevant word lists so the children can check their own work. (If the word lists are to be used only at the end of the game, they should be cut off the photocopied sheet and kept by you until the children are ready to use them.)

◆ a focus question to help children to formalise and begin to make generalisations about what they have just learned.

The title on the left-hand page briefly gives the main learning objective for the activity. The tinted teacher's box in the top right-hand corner of the page also lists information about any prior knowledge children will need in order to play the game successfully. You can use this information as a basis for your introduction to the activity.

The right-hand page contains the letter tiles, playing boards, etc. that children will need. Any other equipment, such as counters and dice, is normally available in a primary classroom.

Adapting the games for differentiation or to teach different letter patterns

The words and letter patterns reinforced in the book are appropriate for most children in Year 4/5 (Primary 5/6) as identified by the National Literacy Framework, although differentiation can easily be achieved in many of the games by giving less able children access to the word lists supplied or by using fewer word tiles. Differentiation, including both additional support and extension, can also be achieved by adapting the games. (Some children may not be familiar enough with the letter patterns taught to play these games. For these children the activities in *Phonics for Reading* and *Words 1* may be more appropriate.) For most of the games, 'player' can mean a pair of children. Children who are less confident at writing, but who can otherwise understand and join in the game, can be paired with children who find writing easier.

Many of the games can also be easily adapted to teach different spelling patterns, or to cater for children who speak with different accents. Simply photocopy the game in the book and blank out the words or spelling patterns you don't want. Once children are confident at playing the games, they may be able to try to create their own games based on some of the formats used here.

Preparing and keeping the games

Most of the games can simply be photocopied, preferably onto thin card, and given to the children to prepare as described. The games can be made to last longer by mounting them onto stiffer card and covering or laminating them. Complete games, including instructions and word lists can then be stored in plastic wallets. Children will benefit from playing many of the games several times each.

Word lists and dictionaries

Some of the games require access to the word lists supplied during the game. The children may also need to use a dictionary (or an electronic spell-checker) to check the spelling of words they wish to use which are not already listed. A rhyming dictionary and thesaurus are also useful, although children will need to know how to use them. Obviously, children will need to be able to use a dictionary, recognising alphabetical order to the fourth letter of a word. Game 1 is provided to help you to assess if children have acquired this skill. All word lists supplied are listed in alphabetical order within relevant categories.

As the children play most of the games they are asked to record the words they make or use so that the spelling patterns or word relationships are reinforced.

At the end of the game they can use the word lists supplied to check their own, or each other's, work. This not only relieves you from the necessity of marking (although it is often useful to at least glance over the children's work), but it gives them the opportunity to reinforce the learning objective and to learn from their mistakes.

Planning a session

A session involving games from *Words 2* may develop like this:

Whole-class work

◆ The teacher introduces, or reminds children of, the main learning objective, be it a spelling or word-making strategy or word meanings. It is helpful at this point to revise areas of knowledge listed under the 'Children should know' heading on the instruction page. It is also worthwhile working through a couple of the examples listed in the game, with the children, using a board or flip chart.

◆ The teacher reads through the instruction with the children, ensuring that they understand what is required of them. The children then re-read the instructions themselves, do any necessary preparation and collect any supplementary equipment (for example, pencil and paper, dice or counters).

Group work

◆ Children play the game, either until the outcome on the list of instructions is achieved, or until a given amount of time has elapsed.

◆ If necessary, children get the word list from the teacher and mark the words collected within the group.

◆ The focus question is intended to encourage the children to focus their attention more tightly on the main point of the activity. These are most profitably discussed within the whole group, rather than by children working individually. They also provide purposeful extension points for plenary sessions.

Plenary sessions

◆ The children talk about the letter patterns or words which they have been using. Encourage children to talk about things which the group disagreed about, or about anything interesting they found out, particularly using the focus question. All the children will benefit from hearing about discoveries others have made.

◆ If required, children can give the piece of paper showing the words they used to the teacher. The teacher can glance at the words used or made and can assess whether the children have assimilated the target point or whether further practice is needed.

Games to teach and reinforce letter patterns and phonological awareness

Many of these games can be played with a whole class, or large group, of children playing together; others are best done within small groups. Supervision by an adult is usually helpful. It is often better, however, if pairs of children work together as one player, particularly if some children find writing hard but are otherwise able to join in. If you have the opportunity to observe the children as they play the games, encourage them to think strategically in terms of letter patterns, not of individual letters.

Shannon's game

(This game is a variation of Hangman, but is better for reinforcing spelling patterns.)

Aim: to guess the word the scribe is thinking of, letter by letter, before the team's 15 lives run out

Size of group: from 3 to 15, in teams, with one scribe in each team

Players will need: a piece of paper and a pencil for each team

The scribe thinks of a word and writes dashes to indicate how many letters there are (for example, thinks of *crocodile* and writes _ _ _ _ _ _ _ _ _). The players in the team take it in turns to guess or work out which letters are in the word and where they occur. (For example, one player might ask 'Is there an *e*'? If the scribe says 'Yes', the player must guess where the *e* is.) If the letter and its position in the word are correctly stated, the scribe writes it in. If not, the team of players loses a life and the scribe writes the letter in a space away from the dashes, circling those letters that are in the word, but whose position was not correctly guessed.

If the players in the team guess the word before their 15 lives run out, they win; otherwise the scribe wins.

Silly sentences

This game can be used to reinforce alliteration (where initial sounds are the same) or assonance (where vowel sounds are the same).

Aim: to say a sentence with a lot of words featuring the same sound

Size of group: 5–6 children

Player 1 says the target sound and all the players must think of sentences to go with the sound. For example:

◆ 'p' at the beginning of *pot* – 'The polite penguin picks up pennies.'

◆ 'a' in the middle of *cat* – 'The fat cat had a cap and a candle in his hand.'

◆ 'i:' in the middle of *sheep* – 'Sheena the sheep has deep dreams when she sleeps.'

This is a co-operative game, and children are expected to help each other out if one makes an error.

Square words

Aim: to make and write down as many words (with three letters or more) as possible in four minutes

Size of group: up to a full class (best working in pairs)

Players will need: a piece of squared paper each with a grid of five squares by five squares marked on it; a pencil

Players take it in turns to call out any letter of the alphabet. As the letters are called out, each player writes one letter in each square on their grid. The players decide for themselves where to write each letter. When 25 letters have been called out (the same letter can be called out more than once), the players have four minutes to find as many words as they can in their own grid. Consecutive letters in the word must be in squares which touch either along a side, or at a corner. So, on this grid, the words *meat, come, comet, team,* etc. would be acceptable, but *cat, came, tome, moat,* etc. would not.

a	m	o		
t	e	c		

The winner is the player who makes most words.

Cross word building

Aim: to make and write as many words as possible

Size of group: 2–4 players

Players will need: a pool of two or three sets of alphabet tiles from sheet 31, face down on the table; a piece of paper and a pencil each

Each player selects seven tiles. Player 1 makes a word, using three or more of their tiles (for example, *tape*), places it on the table, then writes the word on their piece of paper. They then take as many tiles as they have used from the pool, so that they again have seven tiles. If they can't make a word, they choose one of their tiles to swap with a tile in the pool.

Player 2 must now make a word which crosses Player 1's word. Player 2's word can *either*:

◆ have a letter in common with one of the letters in Player 1's word: Player 2 then writes down the word they made (for example, *tool*).

or:

◆ be placed to cover a letter in Player 1's word. Player 2 can alter Player 1's word, but must change it to another proper word. Player 2 then writes down both the word they made (for example, *cake*) and the word they changed (for example, *take*).

E-M-A-T

Aim: to make and write down as many words as possible

Size of group: 2–6, ideally working in pairs

Players will need: one set of alphabet tiles each; a pencil and a piece of paper; a timer

The players should begin with the same four letters each: two consonants and two vowels (for example, *e, m, a* and *t*). (They should be predetermined by an adult who can suggest vowels and consonants which are likely to be productive in word-making activities.) The players should place their tiles face up on the table. They have one minute to make as many words as possible using just those four letters (for example *a, am, at, ate, eat, me, met, meat, mat, mate, tea, team, tame*). They can then add any five letters of their own choice, and they have five minutes to make and write as many more words as they can.

Don't make a word!

Aim: <u>not</u> to complete a word – the player with the fewest points at the end of the game wins

Size of group: 2–6

Players will need: a pool of two or three sets of alphabet tiles, face up on the table; a piece of paper

Player 1 thinks of a longish word (for example, *police*), but doesn't tell anyone, then places the first letter of that word on the piece of paper. Player 2 thinks of their own word beginning with the same letter (for example, *panda*) and places the second letter of their word beside the first letter. The next player must think of a word which begins with the two letters already on the table (for example, *pack*) and contribute the third letter. Play continues until *either*:

◆ one player, intentionally or not, completes a word (for example, they may be thinking of *panda* but inadvertently make *pan*). In which case they get one point.

or:

◆ one player doesn't think there is a word with the letter string on the paper and so challenges the previous player to say the word they were thinking of. If the player cannot state their word, they get a point. If the challenged player can state their word, the challenger gets a point. Remember: the player with the <u>fewest</u> points wins.

Word making and taking

Aim: to complete as many words as possible (within an agreed time)

Size of group: 2–6, ideally working in pairs

Players will need: a pool of two or three sets of alphabet tiles (from sheet 31), face down on the table; a piece of paper

Each player should take a small pile of about 15 tiles. When their pile runs out, they can take some more tiles.

Player 1 looks at their tiles and tries to make a word from them (with at least three letters). If they can make a word, they place it, face up, in front of them. If they can't make a word, they can swap one of their tiles with one from the pool.

Player 2 now tries to make a word. They can

do this either by making a word from their own letters, or by adding letters to Player 1's word and taking it (for example, Player 1 makes *mine*, Player 2 makes *minute*; Player 1 makes *pay* and Player 2 makes *play*.) The only restrictions are that a player cannot simply add an *s* to the end of another player's word.

When it is Player 1's turn again, they can either make their own new word, take a word from Player 2 by adding letters, or amend one of their own words by adding letters.

At the end of the game, players score one point for each word made.

Change the word

Aim: to change a word to a different word in as few turns as possible, each turn involving altering just one letter, but still making a real word.

Size of group: any number, working in pairs

Players will need: a pencil and a piece of paper each

Suggest two words which have the same number of letters (for example, *cat* and *dog*). Ask the pair of children to alter one letter each in turn – still making a real word each time – to change the first word to the second (for example, *cat > cot > dot > dog*). Once the children understand the

game, you can introduce four- or five-letter words. The winner is the player who transforms the words as quickly as possible in as few turns as possible.

Games to reinforce word meanings

These games are quick, 5–10 minute games, which do not involve writing. They can be played with any sized group.

20 questions

This is a familiar game in which one person thinks of an object, tells the others a broad category for that object – traditionally animal, vegetable or mineral, but this can be modified for children, for example a real person, a character in a book, something in the classroom, an animal, something you eat, etc. The rest of the group must ask 'yes–no' questions to determine what the object is. If they can guess by asking 20 questions or fewer, the group wins, otherwise the person who thought of the object wins.

Who am I?

This game is similar in format to 20 questions, but the object guessed must be a person, real or fictitious, dead or alive. Knowing that the answer must be a person helps children to concentrate on descriptive qualities.

PART TWO:
Word games
and instructions

1 Alphabetical order

Number of players: up to four pairs

You will need
- ♦ a copy of game sheet 1, cut up into 48 word tiles
- ♦ a pencil and a piece of paper each

How to play

- ♦ Spread the tiles out, face down, on the table.
- ♦ *Each pair:* Choose ten tiles, keeping them face down. On the command 'Start!', turn over your tiles and start arranging them in alphabetical order.
  The first pair to finish says 'Stop!' You win two points if your ordering is correct.
  Other pairs continue to arrange tiles in alphabetical order until they have finished.
- ♦ *Each pair:* Look closely at your words. Decide who is going to read the first five words (Player A) and who is going to write them down (Player B).
- ♦ *Player A in each pair:* When everyone is ready, pick up the five words (still in alphabetical order) and read them aloud to Player B.
- ♦ *Player B in each pair:* Write down Player A's five words, without seeing them.
- ♦ *Each pair:* Then change round: Player B reads the second five words aloud, and Player A writes them down. Keep playing until you have written down the ten words in alphabetical order.
- ♦ Mark your work, scoring one point for each word in correct alphabetical order and one point for each word which is correctly spelt. (The first pair who said 'Stop!' should add the two points to their score.)

The winning pair is the one with most points.

> **Focus question**
> How many words can you find in your dictionary beginning with *c* which share the same first three letters?

- -

Word list in alphabetical order

above	better	don't	heard	stopped	today
across	between	during	high	such	together
almost	brought	first	knew	suddenly	walked
along	change	found	know	their	watch
always	children	goes	might	there	where
before	didn't	gone	much	those	while
began	different	half	started	thought	white
being	does	head	still	through	without

1 Name .... Date ....

CAMBRIDGE READING

almost	those	walked	started
being	goes	watch	still
their	before	white	know
above	such	might	across
where	began	always	heard
don't	gone	today	better
along	together	brought	children
first	without	does	through
change	during	much	there
while	high	thought	between
different	stopped	head	found
knew	didn't	half	suddenly

2   Two-syllable words with double consonants

Number of players: 2–4, or two teams

You will need
♦ a copy of game sheet 2, cut up into 20 word tiles and 20 double consonant tiles
♦ a pencil and a piece of paper each

How to play
♦ Place all the tiles face down on the table in two separate sets: word tiles and double consonant tiles.
♦ *Player 1:* Turn over two tiles – one word tile and one double letter tile. Say the word it makes if you put the double letter in the middle of the word.
  If it is a real word, keep both tiles.
  If it is not a real word, put the tiles in a discard pile.
♦ *Player 2:* Do exactly as Player 1 did.
♦ Keep playing until all the tiles have been picked up, or no more words can be made. Write down all the words you found. Score one point for each word you made and wrote correctly.

The winner is the player who has made most words and has written them correctly.

Focus question
Which other double consonants can you find in words?

Word list

apple	cotton	pecker
balloon	differ	pepper
better	different	puddle
bubble	dimmer	rubbish
bucket	dinner	sucker
buckle	dipper	sudden
buffet	follow	suffer
bullet	hurry	sullen
cannot	kettle	summer
carrot	mucky	supper
chicken	muddy	tubby
common	mummy	tummy

* If you think you have found another word which is not in this list, look it up in a dictionary.

2   Name   Date

bu		le	ke		le	di		er
pu		le	mu		y	bu		et
pe		er	di		erent	su		en
ba		oon	hu		y	ca		ot
ru		ish	su		er	fo		ow
be		er	tu		y	chi		en
a		le	co		on			

pp	pp	bb	bb	tt	tt	mm	mm
dd	dd	nn	nn	ck	ck	rr	rr
ff	ff	ll	ll				

3 Long and short vowel sounds

Number of players: 2

You will need
- a copy of game sheet 3
- 10–15 counters each (each player will need a different colour of counters)
- a coin with the word 'short' stuck on one side and the word 'long' stuck on the other

- *Player 1:* Flip the coin.
  If it lands with 'long' facing up, read aloud an animal's name which has a long vowel in it. Place one of your counters on top of the name. If it lands with 'short' facing up, read aloud an animal's name which has a short vowel in it. Place your counter on top of the name.
- *Player 2:* Do exactly as Player 1 did.
  If you cannot find an animal's name with the vowel sound you need, miss your turn.

The winner is the first player to make a path from top to bottom or from side to side of the board with their colour counters.

Focus question
How many more animals can you think of with short vowels in their names?

Words with short vowel sounds		Words with long vowel sounds	
ant	hen	ape	mouse
bug	kid	bear	newt
cat	lamb	calf	seal
cub	moth	cow	shark
dog	pig	fly	sheep
duck	rat	goat	snake
fish	swan	goose	toad
fox	wasp	hare	whale
frog	wolf	horse	worm

3   Name   ....   Date   ....

Remember:

● short vowel sounds are the vowel sounds in
  pat, pet, pit, pot, put, putt

● all other vowel sounds are long vowel sounds

goose   ant   dog   goat   bug   fly

hare   ape   calf   wasp   bear   frog

cat   pig   fish   moth   swan   cow

snake   horse   seal   shark   newt   hen

cub   lamb   mouse   fox   rat   sheep

duck   toad   wolf   whale   worm   kid

4   Common letter patterns: *-ight* and *-ought*

Number of players: any number

You will need
♦ a copy of game sheet 4 for each player
♦ a pencil each
♦ a one-minute timer
♦ a dictionary and a rhyming dictionary

How to play
♦ *All players:* On the command 'Start!', begin to write as many words as you can which rhyme with *bright*. You have one minute to do this. Decide how each word is spelt and write it in the correct circle.
If you think of a word which rhymes with *bright*, but has a different spelling, write it outside the circles.
♦ At the end of the minute, compare your answers. If you are not sure of any spellings, look up the words in the dictionary. Score one point for each word you have spelt correctly.
♦ Do the same for words which rhyme with *brought*.

The winner is the player with most points at the end of both sessions.

Focus question
Use a rhyming dictionary to find any other ways of spelling words which rhyme with *bright* or *brought*.

 -

Some words which rhyme with *bright*

-ight
bright fight flight fright height light
might night plight right sight slight tight

-ite
bite kite mite quite site white write

Some words which rhyme with *brought*

-ought
bought brought fought nought sought

-aught
caught taught

-ourt
court

-ort
fort port short sort sport

Words which sound like *bright* and *brought*

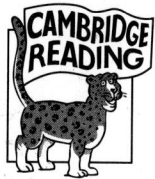

4

Name .... Date ....

In the circles, write as many words as you can which rhyme with *bright*.

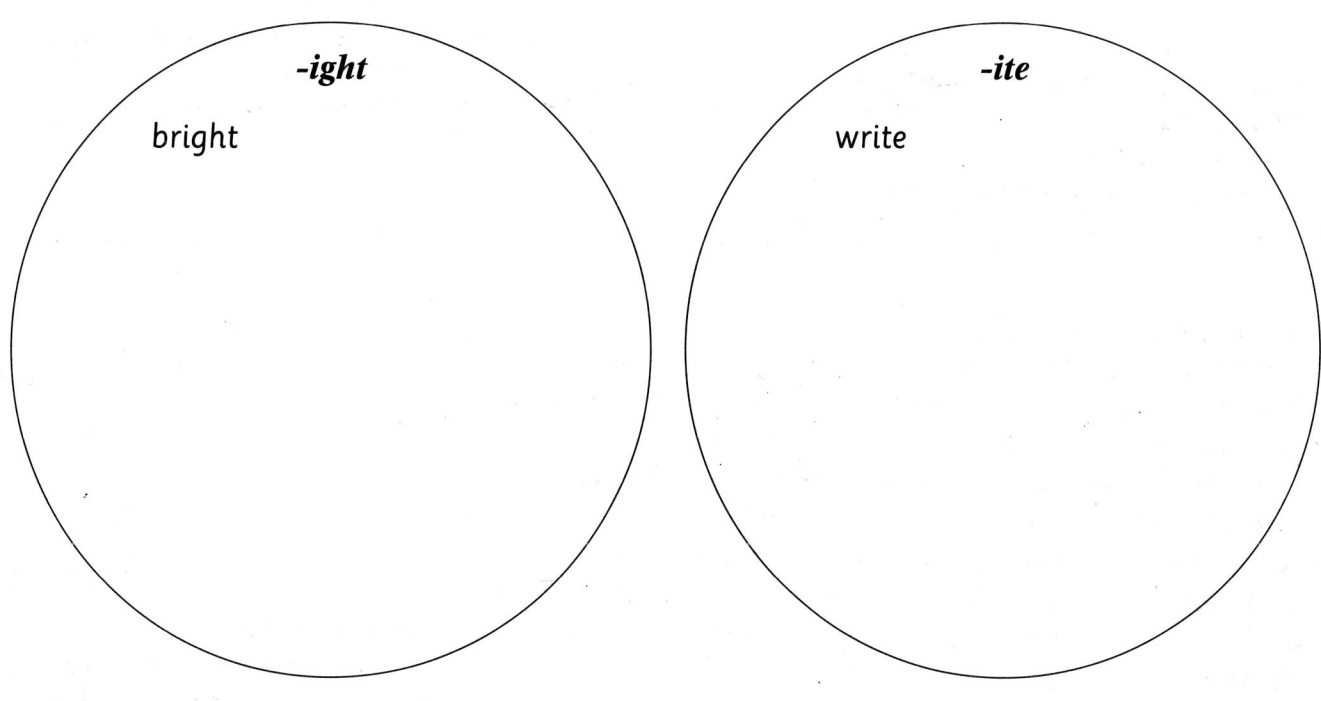

-ight

bright

-ite

write

In the circles, write as many words as you can which rhyme with *brought*.

-ought

brought

-ourt

court

-ort

fort

-aught

caught

5 Different ways of spelling the sound 'k'

Number of players: 2, plus a referee

You will need
♦ a copy of game sheet 5
♦ 10 counters each (each player will need a different colour of counters)
♦ a pencil and a piece of paper each

Before you play
Look at the words in the hexagons below and read them aloud.

How to play
♦ *Player 1:* Decide which hexagon you want to put a counter on.
Say the word that you are trying to make (you will need to add *k, ck, que, c, ch* or *cc*) and write it down on your piece of paper. Show the referee (or Player 2, if you don't have a referee).
If the referee agrees that you have spelt the word correctly, put a counter on the hexagon.
If the referee says you have made a mistake, do *not* put a counter on the hexagon.
Use the grid below, or a dictionary, to check who has made the right decision.
♦ *Player 2:* Do exactly as Player 1 did.

The winner is the first player to make a path from top to bottom or from side to side of the board with their colour counters. All the words must be correctly spelt.

Focus question
Can you make a list which shows all the different ways of writing the sound 'k' in different places in words? For example, does *cke* ever occur at the end of words? Does *ck* occur at the beginning of words?

The completed words in the hexagons are

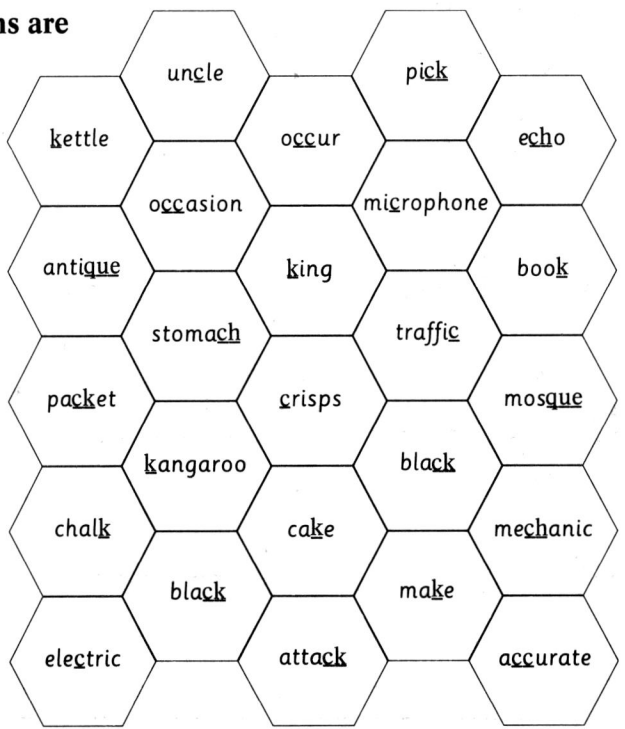

uncle, pick, kettle, occur, echo, occasion, microphone, antique, king, book, stomach, traffic, packet, crisps, mosque, kangaroo, black, chalk, cake, mechanic, black, make, electric, attack, accurate

5 Name .... Date ....

Use *k*, *ck*, *que*, *c*, *ch* or *cc* to finish these words.

un _ le

pi _ _

_ ettle

o _ _ ur

e _ _ o

o _ _ asion

mi _ rophone

anti _ _ _

_ ing

boo _

stoma _ _

traffi _

pa _ _ et

_ risps

mos _ _ _

_ angaroo

bla _ _

chal _

ca _ e

me _ _ anic

bla _ _

ma _ e

ele _ tric

atta _ _

a _ _ urate

6 Different ways of spelling the sound 's'

Number of players: 2, plus a referee

You will need
- a copy of game sheet 6
- 10 counters each (each player will need a different colour of counters)
- a pencil and a piece of paper each

CHILDREN SHOULD KNOW
- *that the sound 's' can be spelt in a number of different ways in different places in a word (for example, ss can never occur at the beginning of a word, whereas ps can only occur at the beginning of a word)*

Before you play
Look at the words in the hexagons below and read them aloud.

How to play
- *Player 1:* Decide which hexagon you want to put a counter on. Say the word that you are trying to make (you will need to add *s*, *ss*, *c*, *ps* or *sc*) and write it down on your piece of paper. Show the referee (or Player 2, if you don't have a referee).
  If the referee agrees that you have spelt the word correctly, put a counter on the hexagon.
  If the referee says that you have made a mistake, do *not* put a counter on the hexagon.
  Use the grid below, or a dictionary, to check who has made the right decision.
- *Player 2:* Do exactly as Player 1 did.

The winner is the first player to make a path from top to bottom or from side to side of the board with their colour counters. All the words must be correctly spelt.

Focus question
Can you list more words which show all the different ways of writing the sound 's' in different places in words?

The completed words in the hexagons are

6 Name _____ Date _____

Use *s*, *ss*, *c*, *ps* or *sc* to finish these words.

a _ k

an _ wer

lo _ _

con _ eal

me _ _ y

mi _ take

almo _ t

_ tarted

_ eiling

fir _ t

le _ _ on

pla _ e

li _ e

_ _ ychology

acro _ _

nece _ _ ary

_ _ issors

al _ o

on _ e

ex _ iting

mi _ _

hou _ e

_ _ ene

_ ircuit

_ econd

Number of players: 2

You will need
- a copy of game sheet 7, cut up into strips of four words
- four coloured pencils (blue, green, red, yellow)
- a pencil and a piece of paper each
- a one-minute timer

CHILDREN SHOULD KNOW
- *that when* g *is followed by* i *or* e, *the sound is usually softened from hard 'g' (as in* goose) *to soft 'j' (as in* gem), *but that there are common exceptions to this rule*

Before you play
Work together, reading aloud all the words on all the strips and using different coloured pencils to underline words, as follows:
   – *blue* for all the words which begin with *g* pronounced as in *gem*
   – *green* for all the words which begin with *g* pronounced as in *give*
   – *red* for all the words which have *g* in the middle, pronounced as in *apologise*
   – *yellow* for all the words which begin with *j* as in *jelly*

As you underline the words, talk about spelling patterns. How do you know the way to pronounce each of the words?

How to play
- Turn all the strips face down and mix them up.
- *Each player:* Choose one strip. You have one minute to look at your words and remember how to spell them. At the end of the minute, hand your word strip to the other player.

- *Player 1:* Read out Player 2's words, one at a time, until Player 2 has written them all down.

- *Player 2:* Read out Player 1's words, one at a time, until Player 1 has written them all down.

- *Each player:* Choose one more strip and look at the words for one minute. Swap strips, then read each other's words out as before.

The winner is the player with most correctly spelt words.

Focus question
Make similar lists of words in which *c* is pronounced as in *cinema*, *curl* and *special*.

✂ -

Words which begin with g pronounced as in gem	Words which begin with g pronounced as in give	Words which have g in the middle, pronounced as in apologise	Words which begin with j as in jelly
general	gear	angel	jacket
genie	get	apologise	jail
gentle	giddy	damage	jam
gentleman	gift	danger	January
geography	gig	energy	jealous
germs	giggle	engine	jet
giant	girl	fudge	jewel
giraffe	give	imagine	jolly
gym	guess	intelligent	juice
gypsy	guide	religion	
		surgery	

CAMBRIDGE READING

7

Name .... Date ....

giant	fudge	girl	intelligent
juice	gentle	surgery	give
giggle	imagine	general	jet
religion	get	jam	giraffe
jolly	germs	gift	engine
gym	jacket	apologise	guess
jealous	angel	gypsy	gear
geography	danger	guide	jail
January	giddy	gentleman	damage
energy	gig	genie	jewel

8　Letter strings *wa-* and *wo-*

Number of players: any number

You will need
- a copy of game sheet 8 for each player, cut up into 19 'word ending' tiles and 37 'word beginning' tiles
- a pencil and a piece of paper each
- a five-minute timer

Before you play
Look at the words in the word list below and read them aloud.

How to play
- Agree how long the game will last. It will probably be about five minutes.
- *All players:* On the command 'Start!', try to make words by combining the word endings with the word beginnings. You need to use each ending at least twice, once with a black beginning and at least once with a white beginning. For example:

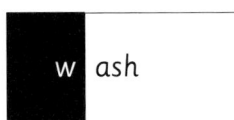 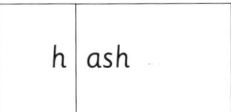

Write down all the words you make.
- At the end of the time, take it in turns to read aloud the words you made. Score one point for every word with a black 'word beginning' tile and one point for every word using the same ending but with a white 'word beginning' tile.
So, *swamp* and *lamp* and *stamp* = 3 points.

The winner is the player who scores most points.

NOTE TO THE TEACHER
This list is subject to regional variation. Please alter the list as necessary so that it is appropriate for the children who are playing the game.

Focus question
Find other words in which you get the letter string *wa-* or *wo-*. Make a list of those in which the *wa-* or *wo-* has an expected pronunciation (for example, *wax*, *wait*, *wok*) and those with an unexpected pronunciation.

Word list

-amp: swamp clamp damp lamp stamp

-ant: want grant pant

-ap: swap bap clap gap lap pap nap yap

-an: swan wan ban clan Dan fan gran nan pan span Stan

-and: wand band grand hand land stand

-atch: watch batch hatch latch patch

-arrel: quarrel barrel

-allow: swallow wallow fallow shallow

-ash: squash wash bash clash dash gash hash lash stash

-ander: squander wander gander grander pander

-arn: warn barn darn yarn

-ater: water grater later

-arm: swarm warm farm harm

-onder: wonder fonder ponder yonder

-ork: work fork pork stork York

-orm: worm form storm

-orth: worth forth north

-orse: worse gorse horse Norse

-ord: word ford lord sword

Name .... Date ....

amp	ant	ap	an	and
atch	arrel	allow	ash	ander
arn	ater	arm	onder	ork
orm	orth	orse	ord	

w	w	w	w	w	w	w	w	w	w
w	w	sw	sw	sw	squ	qu	p	l	h
cl	st	h	b	sh	d	g	gr	f	sp
n	h	f	h	f	d	y			

Number of players: any number

You will need
- a copy of game sheet 9 for each player, cut up into 25 word tiles
- a pencil and a piece of paper each
- a one-minute timer

How to play
- *All players:* Place all your tiles face down on the table and mix them up. On the command 'Start!', turn over all your tiles. Pair up as many as you can where the *-ou-* vowel is pronounced in the same way. You have one minute to do this in.
- *All players:* After the one minute is up, write down all the pairs you have collected. Score two points for each pair you collected and wrote correctly.

The winner is the player with the most correctly spelt pairs of words.

Focus question
How many other words can you find where the letter string -ou- is pronounced in different ways?

- -

Words which are pronounced the same

rough   tough

could   should

route   through

although   mould   shoulder   though

bough   house   mouse   plough   round   sound

flour   hour

cough   trough

four   pour   your

brought   fought

NOTE TO THE TEACHER
This list is subject to regional variation. Please alter the list as necessary so that it is appropriate for the children who are playing the game.

9 Name .... Date ....

CAMBRIDGE READING

rough	could	through	shoulder	mouse
cough	round	four	although	your
brought	trough	hour	flour	though
pour	plough	mould	route	bough
fought	sound	tough	should	house

10 Identifying syllables

Number of players: 2 or 3 pairs

You will need
- a copy of game sheet 10 for each pair
- up to 30 counters for each pair (each pair will need their own colour of counters)
- a pencil and a piece of paper for each pair
- a one-minute timer
- a dictionary

Before you play
Read all the words on the sheet together. Make sure you can pronounce them, and that you know what each one means.
If you are not sure, check in a dictionary.
Clap out the syllables in some of the longer words to remind yourselves of how to divide the words.

How to play
- *Pair 1:* You have one minute to place two, three or four counters on two, three or four words. All the words you cover must have at least one syllable in common with all the other words.

> in+<u>vent</u>
> ad+<u>vent</u>
> pre+<u>vent</u>
> ad+<u>vent</u>+ure

Each of these words has the syllable *vent* in it.

The syllables must *sound* the same, just sharing a spelling pattern is not enough. For example, there are no common-sounding syllables between the words *define* and *definite*.
Write down the words you covered, in their groups, underlining the syllables which the words share. (You do not have to write the words during your minute.)
If you can't find any words which share a syllable during your minute, play passes to the next pair.

- *Pair 2:* When Pair 1 have finished writing their words, do exactly as they did.

- Keep playing until no pair can find two or more uncovered words which have any syllables in common.

The winner is the pair with the most correctly spelt words in groups.

> **Focus question**
> Use a dictionary to look up some of the words you have grouped together. Can you use the word meanings to work out what the shared syllable(s) means. For example, can you find out what *vent*, *tele* and *finite* mean?

CAMBRIDGE READING

10 Name .... Date ....

invent	depress	advent	infect
define	pressure	definite	depart
impress	defect	admire	adventure
prevent	infinite	event	comic
magician	tragic	medical	magical
telephone	microscope	comedy	microphone
electrician	magic	cinema	telescope
medicine	likely	unlike	busy
electric	tragedy	unreal	television
really	dislike	business	electrical

Remember: you are looking for syllables which *sound* the same.

11 -ed and -ing forms of verbs

Number of players: 2

You will need
♦ a copy of game sheet 11
♦ 20 counters each (each player will need a different colour of counters)
♦ a dice
♦ a pencil and a piece of paper each

How to play
♦ *Player 1:* Roll the dice. If you roll a:
- ⚀ put a counter on a word to which you just add -*ing* to make the -*ing* form.
- ⚁ put a counter on a word to which you just add -*ed* to make the -*ed* form.
- ⚂ put a counter on a word in which you have to double the last letter before you add -*ed* (a word with a short vowel followed by a single consonant).
- ⚃ put a counter on a word in which you have to change the *y* to an *i* before you add -*ed* (a word ending in consonant + *y*).
- ⚄ put a counter on a word in which you have to take off the final *e* before you add -*ing*.
- ⚅ put a counter on a word to which you just add -*d*.

Write the word you make on your piece of paper.

♦ *Player 2:* Do exactly as Player 1 did.
♦ Keep playing until one player has crossed out four squares in a row, or there are no empty squares left on the grid (in which case the game is declared a draw).
♦ Check that all the words you have written down are spelt correctly.

The winner is the first person to cross out four squares in a row (vertically, horizontally or diagonally). All the words must be correctly spelt.
(If a spelling error is discovered, the game is declared to be a draw.)

Focus question
Can you work out the rules for adding the suffix -*s* to the base form of a verb?

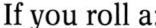

If you roll a:

⚀ **Add -*ing* to make:**
carrying clearing climbing copying crying
frowning happening helping hurrying jumping
laughing licking looking marrying mending
muttering opening packing painting picking
playing pulling sniffing supplying trying
walking watching wishing worrying

⚁ **Add -*ed* to make:**
cleared climbed frowned happened helped
jumped laughed licked looked mended
muttered opened packed painted picked
played pulled sniffed walked watched wished

⚂ **Double the last letter and add -*ed* to make:**
chopped clapped hopped rubbed scrubbed
sipped slapped trapped travelled

⚃ **Change the *y* to an *i* and add -*ed* to make:**
carried copied cried hurried married supplied
tried worried

⚄ **Take off the final *e* and add -*ing*:**
closing cycling hating hoping liking saving
scaring scraping smiling staring using

⚅ **Add -*d* to make:**
closed cycled hated hoped liked saved scared
scraped smiled stared used

CAMBRIDGE READING

11 Name .... Date ....

- Add *-ing*
- Add *-ed*
- Double the last letter and add *-ed*
- Change the *y* to *i* and add *-ed*
- Take off the final *e* and add *-ing*
- Add *-d*

sniff	climb	clap	scare	paint	save	open
laugh	travel	close	cycle	carry	smile	help
like	copy	rub	use	pull	stare	supply
lick	hurry	frown	slap	trap	worry	pick
hope	walk	scrape	scrub	wish	mutter	chop
hop	watch	marry	pack	try	hate	clear
sip	jump	cry	play	happen	look	mend

12 Irregular past tenses

Number of players: any number, playing in teams

You will need
♦ a copy of game sheet 12 for each team
♦ a pencil and a piece of paper each
♦ a dictionary for each team

How to play
♦ *All teams:* Begin at the same time. Fill in all the spaces on the crossword with the present tense form of the verbs in the clues.

Use your piece of paper to try out words, counting their letters, seeing what fits. Use a dictionary to check words if you're not sure of the spelling.

The winners are the first team to complete the crossword correctly, with all the words correctly spelt.

Focus question
How many other irregular verbs can you think of?

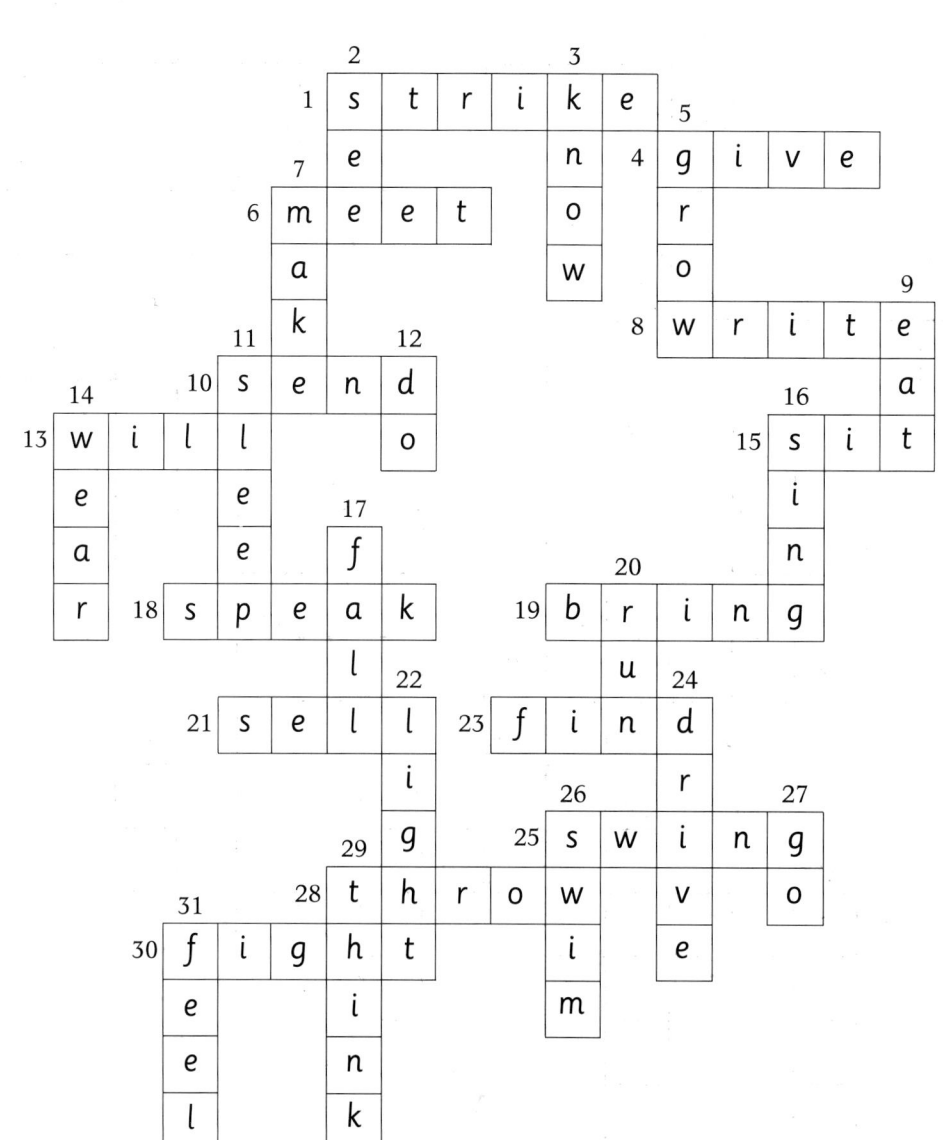

 12 Name .... Date ....

Which present tense form follows *we* or *you*?

Across

1 struck
4 gave
6 met
8 wrote
10 sent
13 would
15 sat
18 spoke
19 brought
21 sold
23 found
25 swung
28 threw
30 fought

Down

2 saw
3 knew
5 grew
7 made
9 ate
11 slept
12 did
14 wore
16 sang
17 fell
20 ran
22 lit
24 drove
26 swam
27 went
29 thought
31 felt

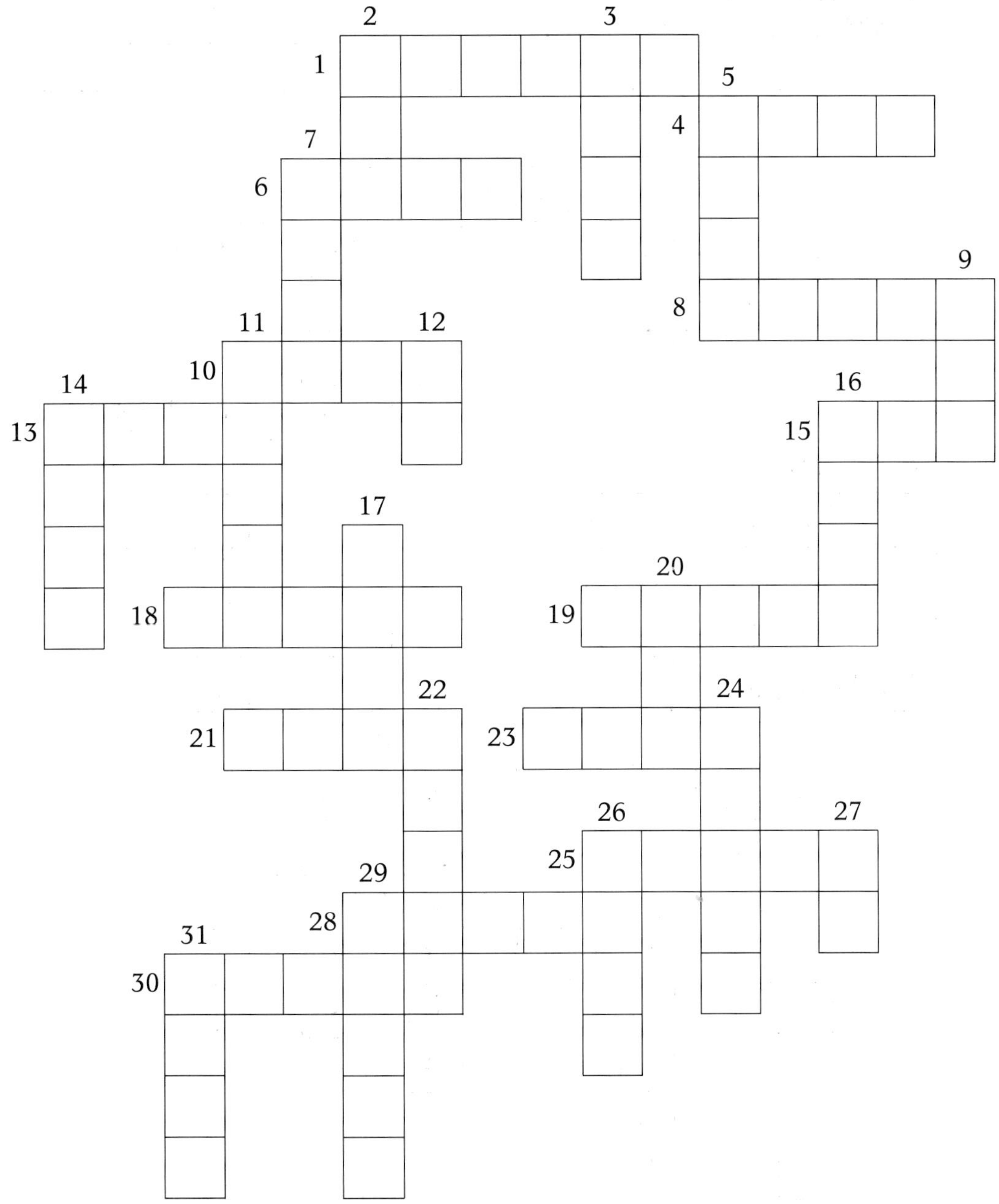

13 Regular and irregular plural forms

Number of players: 2–6

You will need
- a copy of game sheet 13 for each player
- a red, green, blue and orange coloured pencil (or any four different colours) for each player
- a pencil and a piece of paper each
- a timer that will time ten minutes

CHILDREN SHOULD KNOW
- *the rules for making the different regular plurals*
- *that there are other, irregular, ways of making plural forms*

Before you play
Remind yourselves of possible ways of making plural forms:

- Most words simply add an -s (for example, *trains*, *words*).
- Most words which end in a 'hissing sound' (s, x, etc.) add -es (for example, *boxes*, *kisses*).
- Most words which end in consonant + *y* change the *y* to an *i* and add -es (for example, *babies*, *stories*).
- Some words have irregular plurals (for example, *sheep*, *geese*).

> **Focus question**
> How many more words can you find which make their plurals without adding -s?

Use a different coloured pencil to ring each of the different rules for making plural forms.

How to play
- *Each player:* On the command 'Start!', read the nouns on game sheet 13. Decide which way each one makes its plural form and ring the noun with the correct coloured pencil. At the end of ten minutes, you get one point for each word you have ringed correctly.
- *Each player:* When everyone has ringed all the nouns, write all the words and the correct plural forms on your piece of paper.

  You get one extra point for every correct plural form you have made.

The winner is the player with the most points for correct plural forms.

Add -s	Add -es	Change the final *y* to *i* and add -es	Words which make their plural some other way
arrow – arrows	atlas – atlases	baby – babies	child – children
book – books	box – boxes	berry – berries	foot – feet
boot – boots	bus – buses	cherry – cherries	goose – geese
day – days	bush – bushes	fly – flies	leaf – leaves
key – keys	fox – foxes	penalty – penalties	man – men
letter – letters	kiss – kisses	photocopy – photocopies	mouse – mice
light – lights	lunch – lunches	puppy – puppies	myself – ourselves
month – months	match – matches	story – stories	ox – oxen
pen – pens	tax – taxes		person – people
piano – pianos			sheep – sheep
sausage – sausages			wife – wives
school – schools			wolf – wolves
toe – toes			woman – women
toy – toys			
week – weeks			

13 Name .... Date ....

Draw a different coloured ring around each of the ways you can make a plural.
Then use these colours to ring all the words in the game.

Make the plural form by:

• adding -s

• adding -es

• changing the final *y* to *i* and adding -es

• some other way

foot	baby	child	atlas	box
bus	story	book	ox	month
wife	kiss	person	cherry	week
sausage	leaf	fox	match	key
boot	lunch	myself	toe	bush
woman	fly	pen	man	piano
day	goose	penalty	photocopy	school
tax	berry	sheep	puppy	light
letter	mouse	toy	arrow	wolf

14 'f' and 'v' regular and irregular plurals: distribution of 'v'

Number of players: any number, working in pairs

You will need
- a copy of game sheet 14 for each pair
- a pencil each
- a dictionary and a rhyming dictionary for the second activity

Before you play

In your pairs, read aloud the words on the game sheet. Test out what you think the plural of each word is by saying it aloud. Does it have a '-vz' or '-fs' sound at the end?

How to play

- *All pairs:* Start at the same time. Work with your partner and write the plurals in the correct columns.
- When all the pairs have finished, mark the activity, awarding yourselves one point for each correct plural. The pair who finished first can claim one extra point.

The winners are the pair with most points.

> **Focus question**
> Can you work together to complete the second activity? When you have added as many words as possible in each column (use your dictionaries to help you) discuss what you have found out about where you find *f, fe* and *ff, v, ve* and *vv,* in English words.

✂ -

-*fs* plurals   -*ves* plurals

-*fs*	singular	-*ves*
	thief	thieves
	elf	elves
gulfs	gulf	
	dwarf	dwarves
reefs	reef	
	wife	wives
oafs	oaf	
	calf	calves
	knife	knives
roofs	roof	
chiefs	chief	
chefs	chef	
	wolf	wolves
	loaf	loaves
woofs	woof	
	leaf	leaves
	half	halves
hoofs	hoof	hooves
	life	lives
beliefs	belief	

> **NOTE TO THE TEACHER**
> Please check that these plural forms are those used by all the children playing the game – dialects differ!

14 Name .... Date ....

Write the plurals in the correct column.

-fs plurals	-ves plurals	-fs plurals	-ves plurals
	thief thieves		chief
	elf		chef
gulfs gulf			wolf
	dwarf		loaf
	reef		woof
	wife		leaf
	oaf		half
	calf		hoof
	knife		life
	roof		belief

How many words can you find to complete this table?

f-	-ff-	-ff	-f	-fe	v-	-vv-	-vv	-v	-ve
fish fire	suffer office	stiff stuff	thief	not *magic -e*	violin vision	revving	?	?	not *magic -e*
				?					have give
				magic -e safe					*magic -e* five save

15 Common prefixes: *al-, anti-, mis-*

Number of players: 2 or 3

You will need
♦ a copy of game sheet 15
♦ two counters each (each player will need their own colour of counters)
♦ a dice
♦ a pencil and a piece of paper each
♦ a dictionary

How to play
♦ *All players:* Put one of your counters somewhere on the inner, black track and one on the outer, white track.
♦ *Player 1:* Shake the dice. Move each counter that number of squares around its track. You can move in either direction. Combine the prefix on the black square you land on with the word on the white square you land on.
  If it makes a new word, write it down.
  If not, play passes to Player 2.
♦ *Player 2:* Do exactly as Player 1 did.

The winner is the first player to make eight different words.

Focus question
Look at the words you have made. Can you work out what the prefixes *al-, anti-* and *mis-* mean? Try to think of some more words which begin with these prefixes. Look them up in dictionaries to check your answers.

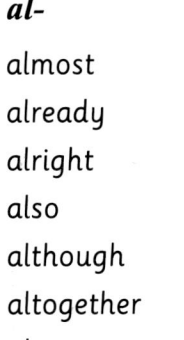

al-	anti-	mis-
almost	anticlockwise	misbehave
already	antifreeze	misfit
alright	antiseptic	mislead
also	antisocial	misplace
although		misprint
altogether		mistreat
always		mistake
		misunderstand
		misuse

Prefixes

15 Name .... Date ....

ready	use	understand	ways	treat
freeze	al-	anti-	mis-	print
though	mis-		al-	right
behave	anti-		anti-	place
clockwise	al-		mis-	so
fit	mis-	anti-	al-	septic
together	take	social	most	lead

Number of players: 2 teams

You will need
♦ a copy of game sheet 16 for each team, cut up into 21 single domino tiles
♦ a pencil and a piece of paper for each team
♦ a timer

CHILDREN SHOULD KNOW
● *what suffixes are and how they are added to the end of words*
● *enough about nouns, verbs and adjectives to recognise that all the words made by adding these suffixes are nouns*

Before you play
Read together all the words in the word list below. Make sure that you can read and pronounce them all. If you are not sure what a word means, check in a dictionary.

How to play
♦ Agree how long the game will last. (This should be between five and ten minutes.)
♦ *Each team:* Put all your dominoes face down on the table and mix them up. On the command 'Start!', turn all your dominoes face up and begin to arrange them in word chains, like this:

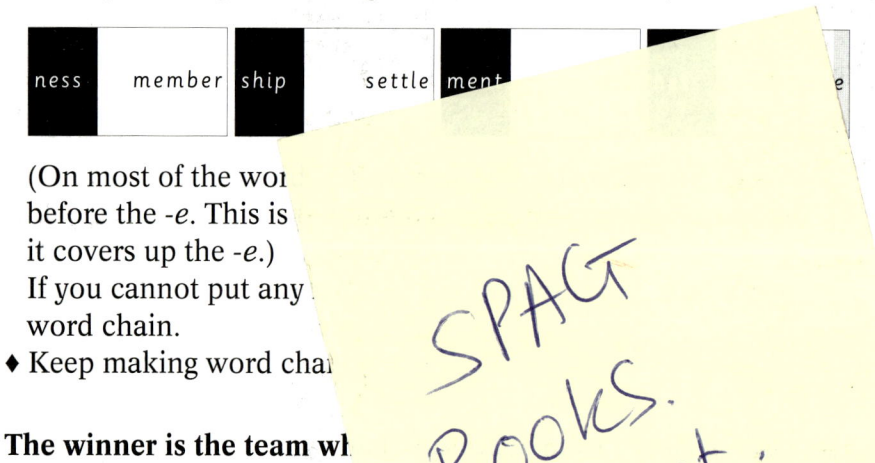

(On most of the wor[...]
before the *-e*. This is [...]
it covers up the *-e*.)
If you cannot put any [...]
word chain.
♦ Keep making word cha[...]

**The winner is the team wh[...]
of the agreed time.**

Focus question
Sort out all the base words on game sheet 16 into word classes: nouns, verbs and adjectives. Which of the suffixes can you add to which word classes?

✂ -

-al	*-hood*	*-[n...]*		*-ship*	*-ation*	*-ist*
arrival	babyhood	am[...]	goodness	leadership	alteration	artist
removal	childhood	argument	kindness	membership	hesitation	cyclist
survival	sainthood	settlement	sickness	relationship	observation	journalist

Suffix dominoes

16 Name .... Date ....

al	observe	hood	arrive	ation	saint
al	argue	hood	remove	ment	baby
al	amuse	ness	survive	ment	kind
ship	settle	ness	member	ment	sick
ship	art	ness	relation	ist	good
ship	cycle	ation	leader	ist	hesitate
hood	journal	ation	child	ist	alter

17 Adjective-making suffixes: *-ful* and *-able*

Number of players: 2 (or two teams of 2)

You will need
♦ the word tiles from the top of game sheet 17, cut up into 30 word tiles
♦ the grid from the bottom of game sheet 17
♦ a different coloured pencil each
♦ a piece of paper each

Before you play
Read together all the words in the word list below. If you are not sure what a word means, check in a dictionary.

How to play
♦ Place all the tiles face down on the table and mix them up.
♦ *Player 1:* Turn one of the tiles face up and read the word aloud. Say the word it makes if you add the suffix *-ful* or *-able*. If it makes a real word, write it down, then cross out one square with that suffix on it.
   Put your word on a discard pile so no-one can use it again in this game.
   If you can't think of how to add a suffix, turn the word over and end your turn.
♦ *Player 2:* Do exactly as Player 1 did.
♦ Keep playing until one of you has crossed out four squares in a row or there are no uncrossed squares left on the grid (in which case the game is declared a draw).
   If all the word tiles are used before anyone has four crosses in a row, re-use the tiles in the discard pile.
♦ Check that all the words you have written down are spelt correctly.

The winner is the first person to cross out four squares in a row and to have spelt the words correctly. The row can be horizontal, vertical or diagonal. (If a spelling error is discovered, the game is declared to be a draw.)

Focus question
If *successful* means 'full of success' and *wonderful* means 'full of wonder', what do you think the other *-ful* words mean?

If *useable* means 'can be used', and *breakable* means 'can be broken', what do you think the other *-able* words mean?

Which sorts of words are the suffixes *-ful* and *-able* related to?

-ful				*-able*		
beautiful	grateful	truthful		acceptable	desirable	noticeable
careful	helpful	useful		admirable	drinkable	reliable
cheerful	hopeful	wonderful		adorable	excusable	removable
dreadful	peaceful			breakable	fashionable	usable
faithful	spiteful			cleanable	honourable	
graceful	successful			collectable	likeable	

17 Name .... Date ....

success	dread	peace	notice	fashion	remove
grace	hope	care	like	admire	collect
use	grate	cheer	rely	desire	accept
spite	faith	truth	break	adore	excuse
beauty	help	wonder	drink	honour	clean

-ful	-able	-able	-able	-ful	-able	-ful
-able	-ful	-able	-ful	-able	-ful	-able
-able	-ful	-ful	-ful	-able	-ful	-able
-ful	-able	-ful	-able	-ful	-able	-ful
-able	-able	-ful	-able	-able	-able	-able
-able	-ful	-able	-ful	-able	-ful	-able
-ful	-ful	-able	-ful	-ful	-ful	-ful

Number of players: any number, working in pairs

You will need
♦ a copy of game sheet 18 for each pair
♦ a pencil each
♦ a dictionary

> **CHILDREN SHOULD KNOW**
> - *that suffixes are letter patterns which can be added to the end of some words to change their meanings*
> - *that some words can be made into adjectives by adding a suffix*
> - *the spelling rules for adding suffixes (see page 10 of the Introduction)*

Before you play
Spend five minutes together reading all the words on the game sheet. Make sure you know what each one means. If you are not sure, check in a dictionary.

In your pairs, agree which suffix you think should be added to the end of each word to change it into an adjective. If you are not sure, check in your dictionary.

How to play
♦ *All pairs:* Begin at the same time. Fill in all the spaces on your crossword by adding a suffix to each noun or verb to make an adjective.

The winners are the first pair to complete the crossword correctly, with all the words correctly spelt.

- -

> **NOTE TO THE TEACHER**
> Some children will need the following information to complete the crossword:

Words that add *-able*
climb – climbable
drink – drinkable
inflame – inflammable

Words that add *-ful*
beauty – beautiful
hope – hopeful
truth – truthful

Words that add *-ing*
amuse – amusing
continue – continuing
interest – interesting
trouble – troubling

Words that add *-like*
child – childlike
life – lifelike

Words that add *-ic*
artist – artistic
athlete – athletic
hero – heroic
history – historic
poet – poetic

Words that add *-worthy*
news – newsworthy
sea – seaworthy

18 Name .... Date ....

Add *-able*, *-ful*, *-ing*, *-like*, *-ic* or *-worthy* to these nouns and
verbs to make them into adjectives.

Across	**Down**
1 interest	2 inflame
5 life	3 truth
6 artist	4 athlete
8 amuse	7 continue
13 trouble	9 news
15 sea	10 drink
16 climb	11 hero
17 hope	12 beauty
18 history	14 poet
19 child	

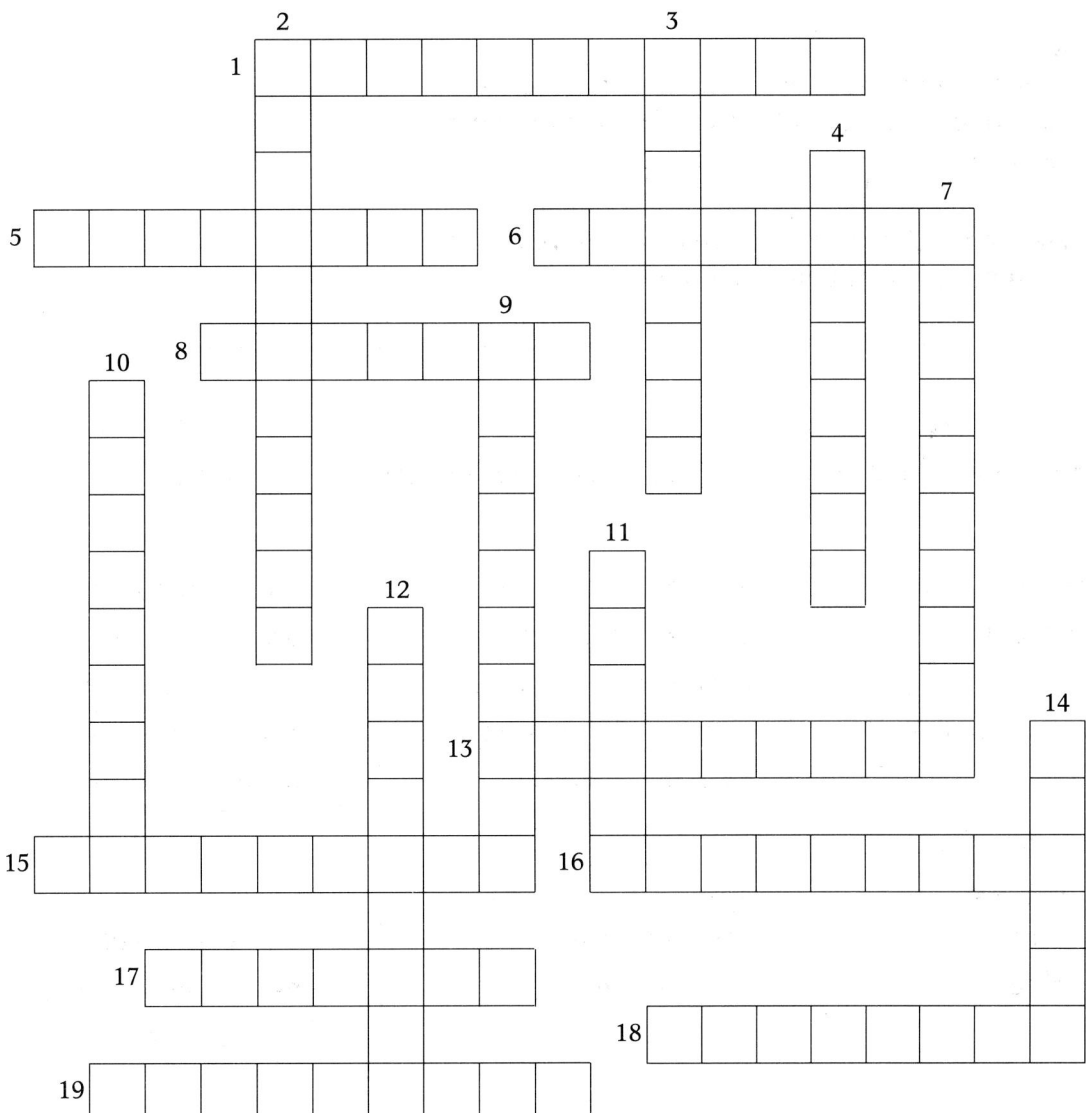

19 Comparative and superlative forms

Number of players: 2

You will need
- ◆ a copy of game sheet 19, with the two wheels cut out and connected with a paper fastener
- ◆ two counters each (each player will need their own colour of counters)
- ◆ a dice
- ◆ a pencil and a piece of paper each

How to play
- ◆ *Both players:* Place one of your counters in any space on the smaller wheel, and the other counter in any space on the larger wheel.
- ◆ *Player 1:* Roll the dice. Move both your counters that number of spaces clockwise around the wheels. Read the base form off the big wheel and the comparative or superlative form off the small wheel. Say the word that this makes. For example:
  busy + superlative = *busiest*
  careful + comparative = *more careful*
  bad + base = *bad*
  Write the form you say on your piece of paper.
  If you don't know the form, or you don't know how to spell it, you miss a turn.
- ◆ *Player 2:* Do exactly as Player 1 did.

The winner is the first person to write ten correct forms, correctly spelt.

Focus question
Can you work out why some adjectives use suffixes to show comparison and others use *more* and *most*? (Hint: look at the number of syllables in the base form and think about stressed syllables).

Find more examples of adjectives to test whether your idea works.

Base	Comparative	Superlative	Base	Comparative	Superlative
bad	worse	worst	heavy	heavier	heaviest
beautiful	more beautiful	most beautiful	helpful	more helpful	most helpful
big	bigger	biggest	hot	hotter	hottest
boring	more boring	most boring	interesting	more interesting	most interesting
busy	busier	busiest	long	longer	longest
careful	more careful	most careful	old	older	oldest
difficult	more difficult	most difficult	sad	sadder	saddest
exciting	more exciting	most exciting	silly	sillier	silliest
fast	faster	fastest	slow	slower	slowest
funny	funnier	funniest	strange	stranger	strangest
good	better	best	strong	stronger	strongest
happy	happier	happiest	weak	weaker	weakest

Making comparisons

19 Name .... Date ....

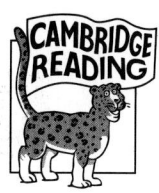

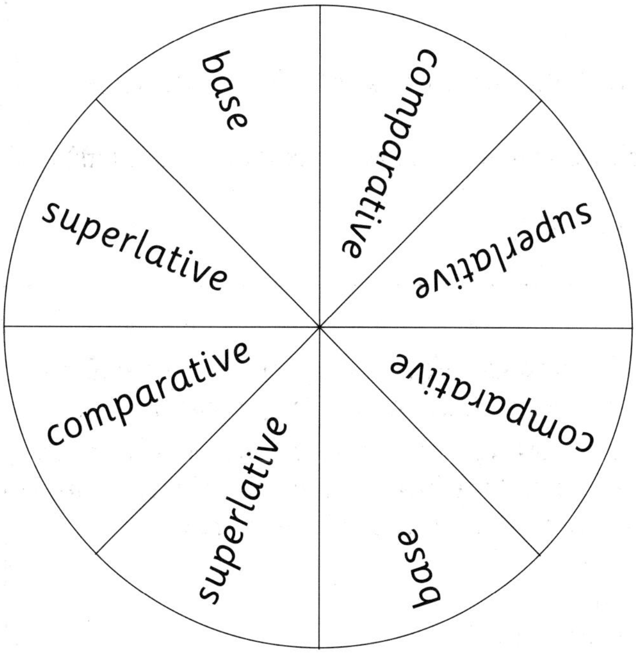

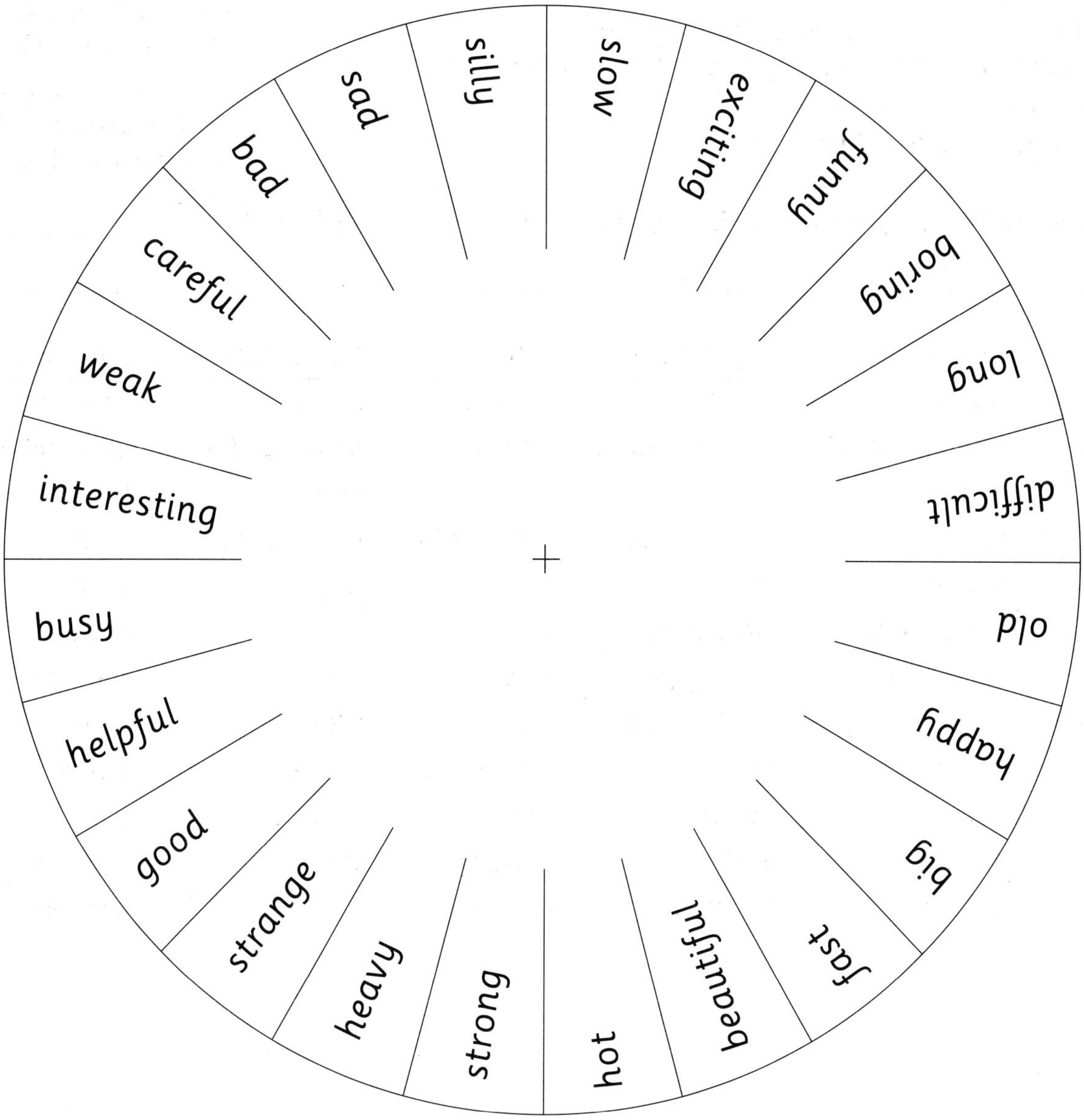

Number of players: 2 or 3

You will need
◆ a copy of game sheet 20
◆ two counters each (each player will need their own colour of counters)
◆ a dice
◆ a pencil and a piece of paper each
◆ a dictionary

How to play
◆ *All players:* Put one of your counters somewhere on the inner, black track and one on the outer, white track.
◆ *Player 1:* Shake the dice. Move each counter that number of squares around its track. You can move in either direction. Combine the prefix on the black square you land on with the word on the white square you land on.
  If it makes a new word, write it down.
  If not, play passes to Player 2.
◆ *Player 2:* Do exactly as Player 1 did.

The winner is the first player to make eight different words.

Focus question
Can you make three more adjectives for each of these suffixes?

-ful	*-ly*	*-ic*	*-ive*
careful	deadly	Arabic	active
cheerful	friendly	artistic	instinctive
hopeful	ghostly	athletic	secretive
painful	lovely	heroic	selective
spiteful	weekly	poetic	
wonderful			

＊ You can also make words like *secretly*, but these are adverbs so don't count in this game.

20 Name .... Date ....

CAMBRIDGE READING

hope	ghost	artist	instinct	week
friend				cheer
pain				hero
Arab				act
spite				love
care				select
secret	athlet(e)	dead	poet	wonder

Suffixes in centre frame:

-ful -ly -ive -ic

-ic ... -ful

-ive ... -ly

-ly ... -ive

-ful ... -ic

-ic -ive -ly -ful

21 Suffixes: *-ible, -able, -ive, -(t)ion, -(s)ion*

Number of players: 4, playing in two teams

You will need
♦ a copy of game sheet 21, cut up into eight cards
♦ a pencil each

> **CHILDREN SHOULD KNOW**
> ● *how to make words by adding a suffix. They should be able to play with words, trying them out to see if they sound right.*

Before you play
Read together all the words in the word list below. If you are not sure what a word means, check in a dictionary.

How to play
♦ Place the eight cards face down on the table and mix them up.
♦ *Each team:* On the command 'Start!', choose a card and turn it face up. Try to make four words by combining the word beginnings and endings. You can only use each beginning once, but you can use an ending more than once. Write the four words you make on the card.
♦ When you have completed one card, turn over another. Try to make four new words using the same rules.
♦ Keep playing until there are no more cards left on the table.
♦ Mark your cards, looking words up in the dictionary if you are not sure whether they are proper words.

The winner is the team with most correct words.

✂ --

Card 1	**Card 3**	**Card 5**	**Card 7**
active	dependable	unsinkable	teachable
action	creative	supportable	flexible
mendable	creation	supportive	decisive
possible	deceptive	reactive	decision
informative	deception	reaction	receptive
information	responsive	terrible	reception
	responsible		

Card 2	**Card 4**	**Card 6**	**Card 8**
invisible	festive	attractive	legible
expressive	formative	attraction	legion
expression	formation	distinctive	captive
fashionable	comfortable	distinction	caption
attractive	irresistible	probable	station
attraction		sensible	uncomfortable

> ✳ If you find any other words, check them in a dictionary.

© Cambridge University Press 1998

21   Name ....   Date ....

1

act	ible	_____
mend	able	_____
poss	ive	_____
informat	ion	_____

5

unsink	ible	_____
support	able	_____
react	ive	_____
terr	ion	_____

2

invis	ible	_____
express	able	_____
fashion	ive	_____
attract	ion	_____

6

attract	ible	_____
distinct	able	_____
prob	ive	_____
sens	ion	_____

3

depend	ible	_____
creat	able	_____
decept	ive	_____
respons	ion	_____

7

teach	ible	_____
flex	able	_____
decis	ive	_____
recept	ion	_____

4

fest	ible	_____
format	able	_____
comfort	ive	_____
irresist	ion	_____

8

leg	ible	_____
capt	able	_____
stat	ive	_____
uncomfort	ion	_____

---

22 Verb families

Number of players: 2–4

You will need
♦ one copy of game sheet 22, cut up into 24 word tiles
♦ dictionaries

> **CHILDREN SHOULD KNOW**
> ● *the meanings of all the words on game sheet 22*

Before you play
Look together at all the words in the family verb lists below. Discuss the meaning of each word. If you are not sure, check in a dictionary.

How to play
♦ Place all the tiles face down on the table.
♦ *Each player:* Pick up five tiles. Try to organise them into families of verbs which have similar meanings.
♦ *Player 1:* Decide which set of words to collect (you must already have at least one word in that set). You can ask another named player 'Do you have any words in the X family?' If they do, they must give all the words in that set to you.
You can then ask another named player 'Do you have any words in the X family?'
Continue your turn until one of the named players cannot hand over a word, in which case they say 'Fish for it'.
Pick up a tile from the table.
♦ *Player 2:* Do exactly as Player 1 did.
♦ *Each player:* As you make a family of four words, put the tiles face up on the table. Each verb family should include one of the words in capitals.
Keep playing until no more verb families can be made.

> **Focus question**
> Can you make more word families like this to make your own game? Use a thesaurus to help you.

The winner is the player with the most verb families at the end of the game.

 -

Verb families

SAID	LAUGHED	WALKED	SLEPT	ATE	SHOUTED
muttered	chortled	strolled	snoozed	munched	cried
stated	guffawed	marched	slumbered	nibbled	screamed
declared	chuckled	strode	dozed	devoured	yelled

CAMBRIDGE READING

SAID	muttered	stated	declared	LAUGHED
WALKED	strolled	marched	strode	chortled
SLEPT	snoozed	slumbered	dozed	guffawed
ATE	munched	nibbled	devoured	chuckled
SHOUTED	cried	screamed	yelled	

23 Spelling and meaning of words that sound the same (homophones)

Number of players: 2

You will need
♦ a copy of game sheet 23 for each player, cut up into 14 word tiles and 14 text strips

How to play
♦ *Both players:* Place all your text strips face down on the table. On the command 'Start!' turn them all face up.

Use the words on the tiles to fill in the gaps on the text strips. You must use all the word tiles and all the text strips.

The winner is the player who fills in all the gaps on the text strips first, using the correct word and making sense.

Focus question
Can you make a list of other homophones and write sentences which show what each of them means? (Start with *your* and *you're*.)

Completed sentences

There are just enough sweets.

We went to the swimming pool. I like it there.

They're busy playing football.

Their mum is very kind./ We like their mum.

Our mum is very kind./ We like our mum!

You are very kind to me.

I have been waiting for an hour.

We have too many cats.

I went to school by bus.

I have two feet.

Can I have a piece of cake?

Adults have peace and quiet when children are at school.

Can you hear that noise?

"Come here!" shouted the woman to the disobedient dog.

NOTE TO THE TEACHER
Beware regional variations in pronunciation of *our, are, hour.*

✂ ---

to	two	too	there	their
they're	our	are	hour	here
hear	piece	peace	there	

✂ ---

[   ] are just enough sweets.

You [   ] very kind to me.

We like [   ] Mum!

I went [   ] school by bus.

Can you [   ] that noise?

Adults have [   ] and quiet when children are at school.

"Come [   ] !" shouted the woman to the disobedient dog.

We went to the swimming pool. I like it [   ] .

We have [   ] many cats.

[   ] Mum is very kind.

Can I have a [   ] of cake?

I have [   ] feet.

[   ] busy playing football.

I have been waiting for an [   ] .

24 Word classes: noun, verb, adjective

Number of players: 2–6, plus a reader

You will need
- ♦ a copy of game sheet 24 for the reader, cut up into 24 word tiles
- ♦ a pencil for each player
- ♦ a piece of paper for each player divided into three columns headed:

Nouns	Verbs	Adjectives

Before you play
All players should look carefully at the words on the game sheet. Check any spelling patterns you are not sure of.

How to play
- ♦ *The reader:* Mix all the word tiles up and spread them out, face down, on the table.
  Pick up one of the tiles, holding it so that the players can't see it, and read the word aloud.
- ♦ *Each player:* Write that word in the column for the correct word class.
- ♦ *The reader:* Keep turning over the tiles, one at a time, reading the words aloud. Give the players time to decide which word class each belongs in and to write the words.
- ♦ Keep playing until all the words have been read aloud and written down.
- ♦ *Each player:* Check your words. Score one point for each word in the correct word class, and one point for each word which is correctly spelt.

The winner is the player who scores the most points.

Focus question
Can you think of at least ten words which can be both nouns and verbs. Write a sentence for each, for example:

I can <u>score</u> goals.

The <u>score</u> was 2–0.

Nouns	Verbs	Adjectives
brother	behave	clever
girl	defend	dangerous
joystick	eat	good
medicine	explode	heavy
mouse	inflate	interesting
scarf	listen	lazy
sofa	see	naughty
tree	write	tall

CAMBRIDGE READING

24 Name .... Date ....

medicine	scarf	mouse	sofa	girl
brother	joystick	tree	eat	defend
inflate	behave	listen	see	explode
write	clever	good	naughty	interesting
dangerous	tall	heavy	lazy	

25 Adjective synonyms

Number of players: 2–4

You will need
- a copy of game sheet 25, cut up into 25 word tiles
- a pencil and piece of paper each
- a three-minute timer

CHILDREN SHOULD KNOW
- *what adjectives are*
- *the meaning of each of the adjectives on game sheet 25*

How to play
- Place all the tiles face down on the table and mix them up.
- *Each player:* On the command 'Start!', choose four tiles and turn them face up. Try to think of one sentence in which you can use as many of your four adjectives as possible. The sentence must make sense. For example, you can say:
  My cat is sweet, cute, friendly and beautiful.
  But you cannot say:
  My cat is sunny, tasty and delicious.
- At the end of three minutes, read your sentence aloud. Score one point for each adjective that makes reasonable sense in the sentence. So, *My cat is sweet, cute, friendly and beautiful* would score the maximum of 4 points.

Play the game three times. The winner is the player who scores the most points.

CAMBRIDGE READING

25 Name .... Date ....

exciting	pretty	interesting	kind	tasty
easy	beautiful	delicious	friendly	sunny
delightful	cool	great	fascinating	charming
mouth-watering	good	delicate	exquisite	sweet
cute	pleasing	generous	okay	excellent

26 Different styles

Number of players: 2–4

You will need
♦ a copy of game sheet 26, cut up into 32 text strips
♦ a copy of the complete texts

Before you play
You can read the complete texts (see below) before the game begins. You cannot look at them again until the game ends.

How to play
♦ *Each player:* Choose one (or two if there are only two players) of the starred strips. This is the first line of your text. Place all the other strips face down on the table.

♦ *Player 1:* Turn over one of the strips. All the players should read the words on it aloud. If the strip is part of your text, pick it up. Otherwise, put it back, face down where you found it.

♦ *Player 2:* Do exactly as Player 1 did.

♦ Keep playing until one of you has picked up all of their eight strips and ordered them into a text.

The winner is the first player to pick up all eight of their text strips and arrange them in the correct order.

Complete texts

*Many years ago,
a fearless knight on his noble steed
rescued a damsel in distress.
The wench was being exploited
by an evil and haughty enchantress.
The youthful couple
took up residence
in a splendid mansion.

*A few years ago,
a brave young man on a horse
saved an unhappy girl.
The poor girl was being made to work hard
by a mean and stuck-up witch.
The young lovebirds
went to live
in a posh house.

---

*The queen would like
you to come
to meet her in her garden.
This important yearly do
is to raise cash
to help to buy
nosh
for the queen's pets.

*By Royal Command
you are hereby invited to attend
a royal reception in the palace grounds.
This prestigious annual event
is a fund-raising occasion
to subsidise the purchase
of necessary comestibles
for Her Majesty's four-legged companions.

CAMBRIDGE
READING

*Many years ago,

a fearless knight on his noble steed

rescued a damsel in distress.

The wench was being exploited

by an evil and haughty enchantress.

The youthful couple

took up residence

in a splendid mansion.

---

*A few years ago,

a brave young man on a horse

saved an unhappy girl.

The poor girl was being made to work hard

by a mean and stuck-up witch.

The young lovebirds

went to live

in a posh house.

---

*The queen would like

you to come

to meet her in her garden.

This important yearly do

is to raise cash

to help to buy

nosh

for the queen's pets.

---

*By Royal Command

you are hereby invited to attend

a royal reception in the palace grounds.

This prestigious annual event

is a fund-raising occasion

to subsidise the purchase

of necessary comestibles

for Her Majesty's four-legged companions.

Number of players: 2–4

You will need

♦ game sheet 27, cut up into 36 tiles

CHILDREN SHOULD KNOW

● *that although there is a general word which refers to all the animals in a family, each sort of animal in the family has a separate word too. The separate word can tell you whether the animal is male or female, young or adult.*

Before you play

Read through the sets of animals on game sheet 27 to make sure that you are familiar with all the words used.

A set consists of the word of the family, the male, the female and the young. The family word (such as *horse, cat, dog*) is set in capitals.

How to play

♦ Place all the tiles face down on the table.

♦ *Each player:* Pick up five tiles. Try to organise them into families of animals.

♦ *Player 1:* Decide which set of words to collect (you must already have at least one word in that set). You can ask another named player 'Do you have any words in the X family?' If they do, they must give all their words in that set to you.
You can then ask another named player 'Do you have any words in the X family?'
Continue your turn until one of the named players cannot hand over a word, in which case they say 'Fish for it'. Pick up a tile from the table.

♦ *Player 2:* Do exactly as Player 1 did.

♦ *Each player:* As you make a set of four words, put your set face up on the table.

♦ Keep playing until no more sets of words can be made.

The winner is the player with most sets of words at the end of the game.

Focus question
Can you think of other ways, using suffixes, which mark whether something is male or female, big or little? For example, *prince* and *princess*, *pig* and *piglet*. Are there any more?

- -

General word	Male adult	Female adult	Young
DOG	dog	bitch	puppy
DUCK	drake	duck	duckling
GOOSE	gander	goose	gosling
COW	bull	cow	calf
HORSE	stallion	mare	foal
PIG	boar	sow	piglet
SHEEP	ram	ewe	lamb
HUMAN	man	woman	child
FOX	dog fox	vixen	cub

27 Name .... Date ....

DOG	dog	bitch	DUCK
gosling	GOOSE	gander	goose
COW	HORSE	cub	vixen
dog fox	FOX	lamb	ewe
ram	SHEEP	child	man
woman	HUMAN	cow	stallion
mare	PIG	boar	sow
bull	calf	foal	piglet
puppy	duckling	drake	duck

Number of players: any number, working in pairs

You will need
♦ a copy of game sheet 28 for each pair
♦ a pencil each
♦ a dictionary

Before you play
Read through all the words in the list opposite. Talk about what they mean. If you're not sure, check in a dictionary.

How to play
♦ *All players:* Begin at the same time and read each definition aloud. Work out what the missing word should be.

If you have difficulty spelling the word, try using your dictionary.

The winners are the first pair to fill in the crossword correctly, with all the words correctly spelt.

❊ The words in the crossword are:

admire   agree   began   come   deliver   eyes

friend   money   people   refuse   sacrifice

school   watch   world   young

Focus question
Can you work with a partner to make your own definitions game? Each make a list of five words and a list of five definitions. Swap them and see if you can match each other's definitions to the right word.

✂ -

The finished crossword should look like this:

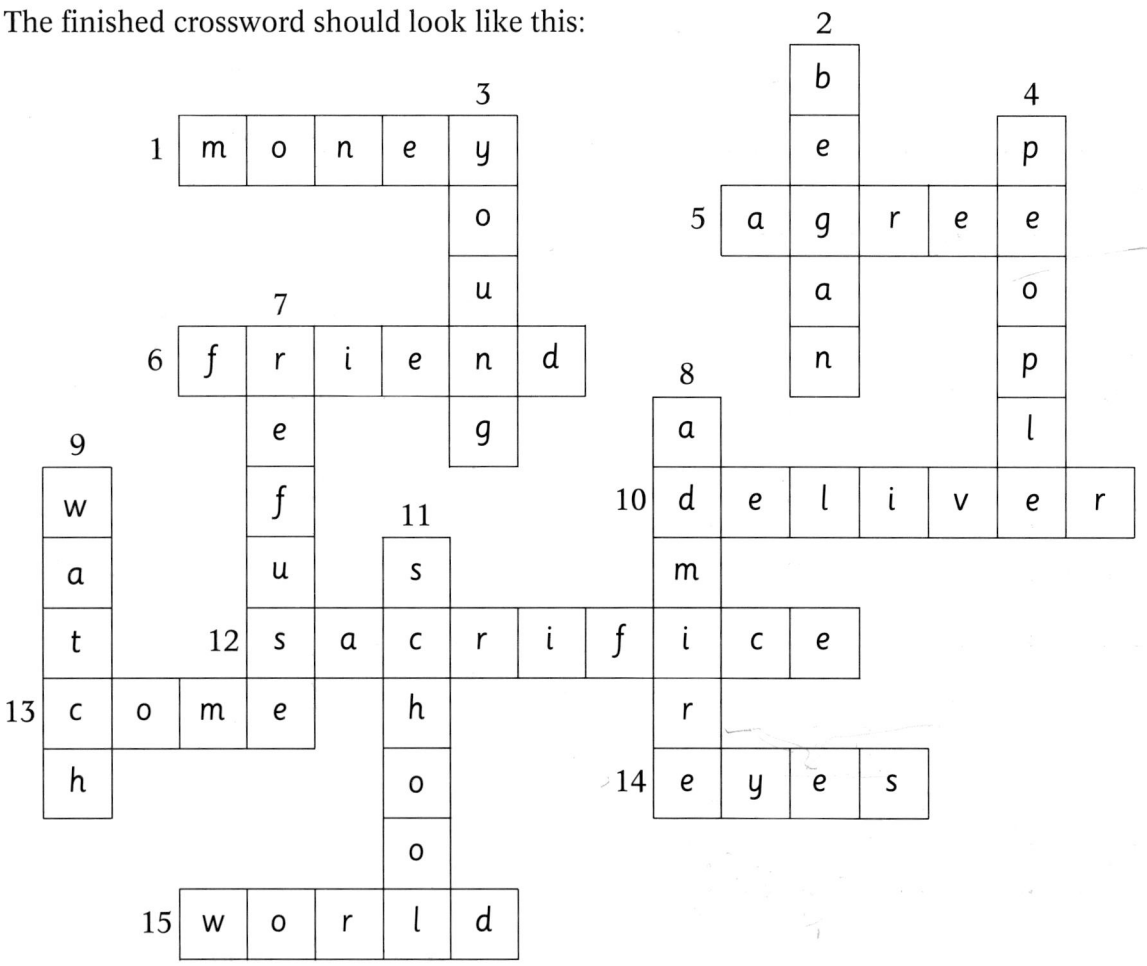

28 Name .... Date ....

Across

1 You use _____ to buy something.

5 If you _____ with someone, it means you are thinking like them.

6 Your _____ is someone like you.

10 If you _____ something, you take it to someone.

12 A _____ is something you would rather keep, but you give it up for a good reason.

13 _____ is the opposite of *go*.

14 You see with your _____.

15 Planet Earth is also known as the _____.

Down

2 The past tense of *begin* is _____.

3 The opposite of *old* is _____.

4 The plural of *person* is _____.

7 If you don't accept something, you _____ it.

8 To _____ someone is to like them and to look up to them.

9 A _____ on your wrist tells you the time.

11 A _____ is a place where children learn.

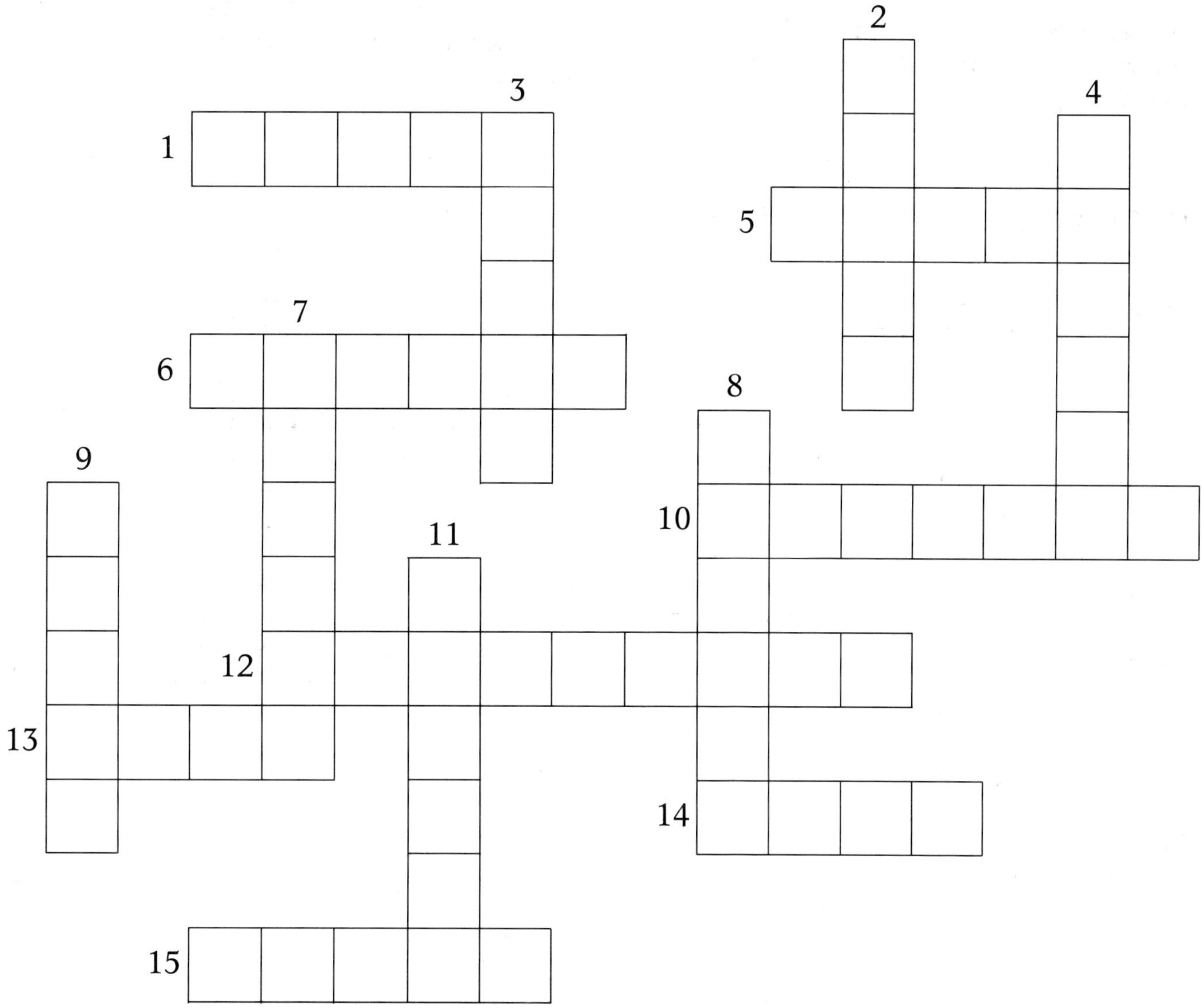

29 Compound words

Number of players: 2 teams or pairs

You will need
♦ game sheet 29 cut up into 27 single domino tiles
♦ a pencil and a piece of paper for each team

How to play
♦ Put all the dominoes face down on the table and mix them up.
♦ *Each team:* Take seven dominoes and turn them face up, but hidden from the other team. Put the rest of the dominoes, still face down, in a pile.
♦ *Team 1:* Place a domino face up on the table.
♦ *Team 2:* Make a word by adding one of your dominoes to one end of Team 1's domino. Read your word aloud and write it down.

   If you can't make a word, say so. When you have had your turn, take one of the dominoes from the pile left on the table.
♦ Keep playing until all the dominoes have been used.
♦ *Each team:* Read aloud your list of words and check that they are all real words.

The winner is the team with most correct words.

> **Focus question**
> In some compound words (for example, *nothing, saucepan* and *cupboard*), each of the two smaller words is pronounced differently from how it would be pronounced on its own. However, if you know the spelling of the smaller words, it helps you to spell the compound word.
>
> Can you find more compound words like these?

- -

Compound word list

anybody	somebody	blackboard	playground
anyhow	somehow	blackout	playroom
anyone	someone	breakfast	plaything
anything	something	classroom	playtime
anyway	sometimes	cupboard	saucepan
anywhere	somewhere	football	underclothes
		footboard	underground
everybody		grandchild	understand
everyday	afternoon	grandmother	underway
everyone	bathroom	grandstand	without
everything	bathtime	handbag	withstand
everywhere	bedclothes	handball	
	bedpan	handstand	
nobody	bedroom	midday	
no-one	beefburger	midnight	
nothing	birthday	midway	
nowhere	blackbird		

29 Name .... Date ....

mother	any	body	after	noon	grand
bag	every	where	beef	burger	hand
ball	no	thing	bed	room	foot
room	some	way	birth	day	bath
out	every	times	black	bird	with
night	some	how	break	fast	mid
time	any	one	class	room	play
pan	cup	board	grand	child	sauce
stand	under	ground	under	clothes	under

Number of players: any number

You will need
♦ a copy of game sheet 30 for each player
♦ a pencil each
♦ a dictionary

How to play
♦ *All players:* Begin at the same time. Read each definition aloud and work out what the word in the crossword should be.

If you have difficulty spelling the word, try using your dictionary.

The winner is the first player to fill in the crossword correctly, with all the words correctly spelt.

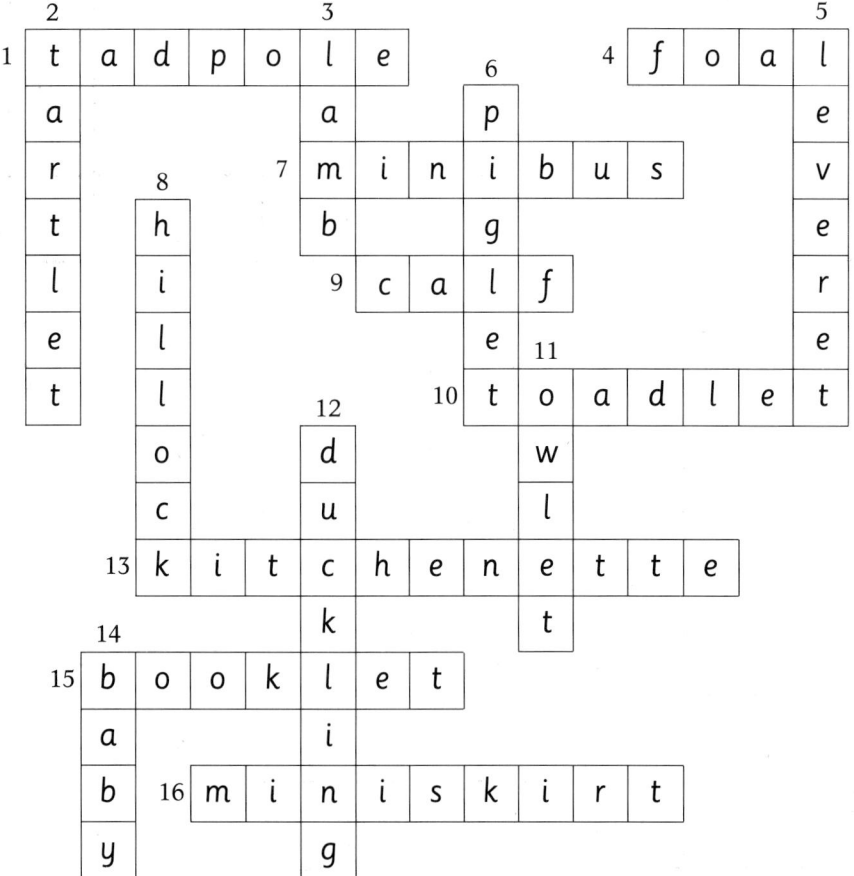

Focus question
Can you sort the words into three columns?
• nouns with prefixes (for example, *miniskirt*)
• nouns with suffixes (for example, *piglet, kitchenette*)
• nouns which can only refer to the small or young thing (for example, *calf*)

Look at the vowels in the suffixes and prefix. Do you see that they are usually short 'i' and 'e'? Think of other ways of changing words to show that the thing referred to is young or small (for example, nicknames like *Tommy, Vicky, doggy*). What kind of vowel sound do you usually find? Can you think of adjectives which suggest that the thing referred to is young or small (for example, *titchy, little*).

Small, young or short!

30 Name .... Date ....

CAMBRIDGE READING

Across
1 young frog
4 young horse
7 small bus
9 young cow
10 young toad
13 small kitchen
15 small book
16 small or short skirt

Down
2 small tart
3 young sheep
5 young hare
6 young pig
8 small hill
11 young owl
12 young duck
14 young child

31 **Alphabet tiles**

a b c d e f g h i j
k l m n o p q r s t
u v w x y z

a b c d e f g h i j
k l m n o p q r s t
u v w x y z

a b c d e f g h i j
k l m n o p q r s t
u v w x y z